More praise for
'Boy in the Mirror'

*Bartko's courage in speaking out to the sports world and beyond
provides support for all who work to protect kids.*

JEFF ANDERSON,
AMERICA'S LEADING CHILD-ABUSE ATTORNEY

*In a world where the courage of adults seems to be lacking, Jim
Bartko gives his reader a deeply vulnerable account of how childhood
trauma often manifests in life. And yet Bartko simultaneously inspires
us with his resiliency. This book gives the reader both permission, and
the language we need, to talk about an extraordinarily uncomfortable but epidemic topic. Through the sheer power of Bartko's story,* Boy
in the Mirror *motivates its readers to learn more about prevention and
survivor advocacy—and inspires us to have greater empathy for each other.
Because you never know who is suffering in silence.*

KATELYN BREWER,
PRESIDENT AND CEO, DARKNESS TO LIGHT,
A NATIONAL ORGANIZATON DEDICATED TO HELPING STOP CHLD SEXUAL ABUSE

With Boy in the Mirror, *Jim Bartko has borne his soul for the benefit of
others. Jim's remarkable story is as riveting as it is heartbreaking and cathar-
tic. It is difficult to comprehend the challenges and everyday battles that are
the center of this self-reflective and insightful book. I congratulate Jim for his
strength, courage, and willingness to share his journey.*

BOB BOWLSBY,
COMMISSIONER, BIG 12 CONFERENCE

*In Jim Bartko's domain of big-time college athletics, the most
celebrated individuals are called "game-changers." But the
publication of* Boy in the Mirror— *his deeply personal and startlingly*

vulnerable account of the effects of childhood sexual abuse and untreated trauma that so many men hide beneath outward displays of bravado— makes Bartko into something more: a world-changer."

JACKSON KATZ, PH.D.,
AUTHOR OF "THE MACHO PARADOX"
AND CREATOR OF THE EDUCATIONAL DOCUMENTARY
"TOUGH GUISE: VIOLENCE, MANHOOD AND AMERICAN CULTURE"

Jim's book should be read by everyone with a career in child abuse prevention and treatment. More importantly, it is a must read for all parents and other adults who need to become much more aware of how trusted adults in their communities groom, and then abuse, children they know, and how they can help prevent this crime from continuing to occur.

SID JOHNSON
FORMER PRESIDENT AND CEO,
PREVENT CHILD ABUSE AMERICA

Boy in the Mirror

Boy in the Mirror

An Athletic Director's Struggle
to Survive Sexual Abuse as a Child

Jim Bartko

with Bob Welch

DAJ Publishers

DAJ Publishers

Front cover: Drawn by Tinker Hatfield, Nike's Vice President for Design and Special Projects.

Front and back cover designs by Bob Welch and Tom Penix.

ISBN: 978-1-7346683-0-8

To contact the author: boyinthemirror@gmail.com

Printed in the United States of America

To the friends and family members
who have supported me through the storm.

And to the other boys and girls in the mirror, with honor
for their courage and hope that my story might unlock their own.

Table of Contents

My barn having burned down, I can now see the moon.

MIZUTA MASAHIDE,
17TH-CENTURY JAPANESE POET AND SAMURAI

Foreword

I've known Jim Bartko for more than twenty-five years. During that time, he has been a top-notch collaborator and a loyal and steady friend. His upbeat, creative, and go-go-go personality helped drive the reimagining and rebranding of the University of Oregon. His work—in tandem with great coaches, and a bit of help from Nike—drove UO's sports programs to ever higher levels of excellence and success.

Little did any of us know that he had been, since childhood, waging a battle for his soul. For happiness. When his story came out and he decided to write about it, I was honored to be asked to create an image for the cover.

The drawing is quite possibly the most emotional piece I've ever done. To think of Jim as a helpless and sad little boy required reading the book and then going to my own dark places to try and understand the embarrassment and unending hurt that has ripped him throughout the years, day and night.

I chose blue for the tie because it is the official color for sexual abuse awareness and prevention. More importantly, I depicted an emerging "glow" shining on little Jimmy because despite the oppressive darkness, there is hope and there is light, in the form of treatment and watchful prevention.

There is always a chance for light and happiness.

This book is an amazing testament to Jim's resilience, willingness to seek help, and desire to help others.

Tinker Hatfield

Note: Hatfield is Nike's Vice President for Design and Special Projects. In 1998, he was chosen by Fortune *magazine as one of the "100 Most Influential Designers" of the 20th century. Among his many shoe designs are the Air Jordans III through XV, XX, and XX3, and the Air Pegasus. A former pole vaulter at the University of Oregon, he was, in 2008, inducted into the Oregon Sports Hall of Fame for his "Special Contribution to Sport."*

Author's Note

This book interlaces two subjects: college sports and childhood sexual abuse—my own. For me, the two are inextricably linked. My abuser was a priest who served as my youth basketball coach. Like a sinister shadow, the trauma resulting from that abuse followed me wherever my career in athletics took me. And the harshest period of my life included being forced to resign as a Division I college athletic director—coincidentally or not, shortly after I went public, in 2017, regarding my abuse.

Beyond that, the power of sports helped me get through many of the tough times since the abuse began—from imaginary baseball games I'd play as a little boy to University of Oregon athletics that have consumed much of my adult life.

Never before have leaders in the realms of professional, college, and high school athletics teams paid more attention to the value of mental health as it relates to sports. As well they should. For too long, athletes have hidden personal struggles, in part to live up to the idea that they must not show weaknesses. Finally, our society is starting to realize that being open about your struggles is anything but a weakness.

Personally, I can't be open and complete about my life without going deeply into both subjects—sports and abuse. It's my hope that readers particularly interested in one of those subjects will be enlightened by the other.

Jim Bartko
Eugene, Oregon
March 2020

Prologue

At Nike's plush headquarters in Beaverton, Oregon, in a room not far from Lake Nike and a shortened replica of the eighteenth hole at Pebble Beach, waiters bustled to and fro in preparation for the gala dinner that was soon to start. It was August 2007.

Outside, as guests arrived, the warm day had cooled to a perfect early-evening temperature. Not far away, the University of Oregon Ducks football team headed for the locker room after holding a special practice session at the headquarters of the company co-founded by the UO's most famous alum, Phil Knight.

Inside, Frank Sinatra's "Fly Me to the Moon" seasoned the setting with an upbeat ambiance. A dozen tables festively decorated in Oregon's school colors, green and yellow, awaited the carefully chosen guests who now sipped drinks, laughed, and snacked on hors d'oeuvres.

I passed. By now, my stomach was churning like the McKenzie River's Marten Rapids. This, after all, was my gig as UO's executive senior associate athletic director; succeed and there'd be back pats and toasts and, more importantly, a major step forward for the University of Oregon; fail and there'd be doubt and behind-the-back whispers and a missed opportunity for the UO to take that giant step.

We'd invited only sixty people to what we called "The Golden Age of Oregon Athletics." It was a carefully selected group whose common denominator was this: Each had a deep love for the University of Oregon and deep pockets to help the school become greater than it already was. This was a virtual "who's who" of blue-chip UO donors, some of whom had arrived in Portland on private jets.

Our goal? To raise money for a new basketball arena to replace McArthur Court, which was lovable to aging alums but laughable to eighteen-year-old hoop recruits who preferred a bit more glitz. But, more importantly, to make sure Phil and Penny Knight understood how deeply their financial contributions to—and love for—Oregon had been appreciated.

Over the years, I'd noticed that outsiders, when hearing of the Knights, thought of only one thing: money, money, money. In so doing they missed the essence of this extraordinary couple: their passion to help the institutions they loved—be it UO, Stanford, or the Oregon Health & Science University (OHSU)—and the people who are served by those institutions.

From across the room, I nodded a smile to UO President Dave Frohnmayer and his wife, Lynn. I glanced at my watch—show time in twenty minutes—and ducked into the bathroom. Had I forgotten anything? Along with the ample help of Downstream, a company specializing in creating design experiences, it felt like I'd been the choreographer for the Super Bowl halftime show. Lights. Videos. Dinner. Drinks. Guests. Speakers. Everything had been carefully orchestrated for what we hoped would be a historic night for the UO. In essence, the gathering had been about ten years in the making—and its success or failure was pretty much going to make or break me.

As I often did when feeling the pressure, I leaned over and splashed water in my face. When returning to the upright, locked position, I looked in the mirror. There I was, Jimmy Bartko: Forty-two years old. Husband. Father. Friend. An influencer of a Division I athletic department. And by some measures, I suppose, a successful man.

After all, wasn't I standing in the world headquarters of the largest supplier of athletic shoes and apparel on planet Earth? And seven years ago, hadn't it been my job to help win back Knight, the head of that company, after he and his alma mater had a falling out? With a whole lot of help, we'd done so. Now, with hopes of revamping the northeast corner of the campus—the university's most highly visible stretch along busy Franklin Boulevard—with a new arena, we knew that Phil and Penny's involvement could jump-start the project.

But by now I'd learned that you didn't engage the Knights by holding out your hand. Instead, you did so by reminding them of the wonderful university that they'd helped sustain. By painting the story with context—Phil having run track for Nike co-founder Bill Bowerman and earned a business degree at UO in 1959. By emphasizing the Duck family of which the two were such an integral part. And, most importantly, by having a solid plan to find success.

I was confident the evening would achieve that—OK, guardedly optimistic. But two things had my stomach in knots. One was the athletic adage that no victory is assured until the clock ticks to zeroes. The other was a secret I'd harbored now for more than three decades, a secret that every time I looked in the mirror, I longed to believe I could forget—but couldn't. It followed me.

Every.

Single.

Day.

It was like a vulture of past shame and future doom that I could never quite outrun. And none of my friends or family knew about it. None. What had happened to me as a kid was an emotional one-two punch, the violations representing the first punch and my silence about them the second. It wasn't bad enough to have gone through what I did. The salt in the wound was feeling guilty for harboring a secret that, even if I hid it for all the right reasons, only deepened my shame. And it meant that not only could I never quite heal, but I could never get through a day—even with my mind riveted to a huge event like this one—without a flashback, or five or ten.

My cell phone quacked with the Duck ring tone. The name on the screen only ratcheted up my angst: "Phil Knight."

"What's up, Phil?" I asked.

All I heard was coughing. Coughing seemingly without end. Then came what sounded like a voice from the dead. No, not a voice, more like a rasp, like a guy who'd been shot and was saying his final goodbye.

"Jimmy," he said, "I'm … so … sorry. Killer … cold. Maybe even flu."

"You're kidding, right?"

"Temperature's nearing triple digits and—"

This must be some kind of joke, I told myself. He and Penny were the guests of honor. The whole event hinged on them.

"We wanted to be there, Jimmy. Honest."

"Seriously, you can't come?"

"I'll text you some notes you can read," he said. "Sorry, Jimmy, best I can do."

The line went dead.

I stood there, frozen by fear, only thawing to shake my head in disbelief. This couldn't be happening, could it? The whole idea was to honor Phil and Penny and, in so doing, to inspire others about giving to the university we all loved.

With panic in my step, I returned to the room where people were still schmoozing with drinks and hors d'oeuvres in their hands. I offered a nervous on-off smile to Pat Kilkenny, the athletic director who had had—and would continue to have—a huge impact on the rise of Oregon athletics. Around me, motion swirled everywhere. But I stood as still as someone in a photograph. Stymied. *What to do? Who to tell? Where to go from here?*

Suddenly, I felt a tap on my shoulder. I turned around. There were Penny and Phil Knight, the latter of whose devious smile quickly morphed into an outburst of laughter. He lifted his glass to me in a mock toast. He appeared to be in the picture of health, looking particularly sharp in his sports coat, slacks and, of course, black Nikes.

"Good evening, Jimmy!" he said.

"What the hell?"

He smiled large and raised his eyebrows as if to say: *Gotcha!* I shook my head sideways as he pulled me into a handshake-turned-hug.

"Brilliant," I said, rolling my eyes and then laughing myself. "Hook, line and sinker."

He laughed as a means of celebrating his mischievous success. Turns out Knight had made the call from a nearby office, then scurried out to rejoin the party. At the moment I was too stunned to put the prank into perspective. Only later would I realize that for some strange reason the guy considered me a good enough friend to dare to pull a fast one on.

BY NOW, THE cultural norm at Oregon, at least in athletics, had become one of swimming against the current, daring to take risks, and refusing to do things just because "everyone else did it this way." And it was working. Once an athletic afterthought in America, the University of Oregon was emerging as a bona fide player. A football team that had been, in the 1970s, among the worst in the country, had risen to No. 2. Enrollment at the school was soaring.

Given our penchant for not following the crowd, we decided to reverse the batting order for the program: speeches, then dinner. I walked to the podium, scanned the audience, and offered my opening remarks. I liked the energy in the room. I liked the get-right-to-business-before-eating approach. I liked that among the eyes I saw as I scanned the room were those of Penny and Phil, a guy who, fifteen minutes ago, I thought was MIA.

"In the last two decades, the University of Oregon has emerged as a true player among American universities," I began. "And yet there are higher mountains to climb in our attempt to achieve more in terms of athletics and academics. Tonight, we want to share with you our vision about one such mountain—our dream to build a new arena, not to ignore the older alums who love what we already have in Mac Court but to embrace the young athletes who are our future."

President Frohnmayer shared his vision for the university and the integral part athletics played in it. E. George Hosfield, the financial manager of the project as part of Ferguson Wellman Capital Management, offered remarks. Kilkenny, the AD, welcomed our guests. Then I got up again, this time to introduce our guest of honor. I reminded myself to be patient; I can be a literal fast-talker, at times with a slight stammer.

"And now I want to turn the microphone over to a man who, along with his wife, Penny, has done … so … much … ." I saw the two in the crowd. "I've come to realize just ... how ... special ... you … ."

I froze in mid-sentence. My unexpected emotion might have startled the crowd. It certainly startled me. Looking back, I think that night was something of an epiphany for me, as if the go-go-go pace of my time at Oregon had precluded me from putting my relationship with Phil and Penny into perspective. As if I were being reminded of what a privilege it was to not only be part of the Oregon family, but to be genuine friends with two of the most decent—and, at times, most misunderstood—human beings on the planet.

"We love you, Jimmy!" someone yelled.

That remark helped. Although I could be seen as confident, deep down, my childhood experiences had programmed me to doubt myself. I finished the rest of my introduction, greeted Phil with a handshake that turned into a hug, then sat back and listened to one of the finest speeches I've ever heard. Though he is, by and large, a private man, I've heard Phil give numerous speeches. None was better than this one. And the audience realized it. The raucous atmosphere quieted to a hush of reverence. More than a few people's eyes glistened with tears, mine included.

He talked of how much his business degree from the school in 1959 had helped him, along with Bowerman, launch Nike. Of the pride he took in knowing that thousands of students were benefitting from the Knight Library and Knight Law School. And of the greatness of the UO as a whole.

But he spoke of how much greater the school could be if people stepped up and gave more. He talked of the wonder of dear old Mac Court, a cramped, outdated basketball arena—the second oldest on an

America campus—but cautioned that history taught if we dare not risk and grow, we die. He talked of how Bowerman's voice "still rings clear in my mind. Without Bill Bowerman there'd be no Nike. Without Nike we wouldn't be here tonight."

Now, as Phil drilled deeper into the hearts of these folks, I realized this was like nothing I'd ever seen. It was beyond dollars and cents. Beyond donations. Beyond tax write-offs. The giving was only a manifestation of the deeper stuff of the heart, in this case, said Phil, of our bonding with a university we loved.

"And with that," he said, "I want to announce that Penny and I are stepping forward to establish what we'd like to call the UO Athletics Legacy Fund. We will be giving $100 million"—a few in the audience gasped—"to help repay the bonds for the construction of the 12,541-seat arena that Oregon will soon break ground on."

The crowd erupted in applause. I sat and took it in with a sense of wonder. Stunned. Ecstatic. Inspired. Nobody felt as much respect for a man who, seven years before, had left the UO fold deeply hurt over what he saw as a slight to his company. That's because after the Phil-UO split it had been my unofficial job to help us not sever our relationship with him for good. Somehow, with lots of help, we'd managed to do so—after nearly seven months. Not by coercion. Not by flattery. But by remembering what this is all about: relationships.

The Knights' gift on this magic night was the largest single donation to UO in the school's century-plus history—for a $200 million building that would be the most expensive on-campus arena in the country. (Their giving to the university wouldn't end there; a decade later their $500 million gift for the Phil and Penny Knight Campus for Accelerating Scientific Impact would, said UO President Michael Schill, lead to "a seminal moment for the University of Oregon, an inflection point that will shape the trajectory of the university for the next century and beyond.")

Somehow, I came to realize, a tiny slice of this feel-good pizza belonged to me, a chance to be part of a university that, if not re-inventing itself, was propelling itself to all-new academic and athletic heights and becoming a national brand. That's what I loved about sports—the way they could bring together all sorts of diverse people for the common good.

From the audience, more cheers resounded. More enthusiasm. More people mentally reaching for their checkbooks.

This, I realized, might be to university advancement what defensive back Kenny Wheaton's interception against Washington was to UO football advancement in 1994: a single play that could change everything. With the momentum of the new arena and a new alumni center next door, what galaxies could the Ducks fly to beyond this? What academic dreams could we identify and go after? What worlds could we yet conquer?

The rest of the evening played out in my mind as if in slow motion. Now, more than a decade later, I count the event as among my Mount Everest moments. It was a reminder of how sports can stir the wonder of the university's academic side. Of how people can use their power for good, be it helping a no-confidence kid earn a college degree, an OHSU patient beat cancer, or an athlete who grew up on the streets of Compton, California, find a new sense of community.

"Nice work, Jimmy," someone said as they bid me farewell.

"What a night," said another. "A game changer. Good job, Bartko."

When the last of the guests had gone I just stood there with a smile on my face, amazed at how we'd accomplished exactly what we'd set out to do. I bid farewell to Phil, Penny, and friends, promising to join them shortly for a drink at a local watering hole.

Frankly, the moment felt good. Real good. Ever since I was a kid, I'd loved playing on athletic teams and loved those moments when I knew I'd done something to help us win.

That's exactly how I now felt.

I quickly slipped into the same restroom I'd hit before the event. Suddenly, my "up" mood crashed down like a runaway elevator. There he was again: the man in the mirror morphing into the boy in the mirror. That's how it always worked. I could get lost in an event, a game, a season, a fundraising campaign—and all but forget the other side of who I was. But then something would happen to trigger the memories. I'd see a priest, see a basketball slammed into a wall or, in this case, see my face in the mirror, and it was as if the son of a bitch had won again.

I'd remember how I was sexually abused as a kid.

*   *   *

By 2019 THE number of priests who've sexually abused children had grown to 6,846, according to the United States Conference of Catholic Bishops. They abused more than 19,000 children—and these are only the cases that were reported.

The problem, of course, goes far beyond the Catholic church, to the Boy Scouts of America, which, in February 2020, filed for bankruptcy because of the number of lawsuits brought against it by survivors of childhood sexual abuse; to universities, among them Penn State and Michigan State; to churches in general; and to an array of other institutes—the kinds of places we used to trust. The National Center for Victims of Crime estimates one in five girls and one in twenty boys has been a victim of child sexual abuse. And nine out of ten who were assaulted knew the person who molested them.

This book is about one such person: me. I've seen the fallout firsthand, lived the shame, watched as my career and marriage fell apart—all because of something rooted decades ago that was not my fault. Even in the best of times, like the evening we honored Phil and Penny Knight, the haunting memories can show up in the mirror.

To tell my story is to undo nearly fifty years of silence. And it's to set the record straight about who I am. In mid-2019, people Googling my name found a Wikipedia entry that included the following lines regarding my time as athletic director at Fresno State University: "Bartko took office on January 1, 2015. He resigned abruptly as athletics [sic] director on November 6, 2017, due to struggles with alcoholism and a domestic separation."

I prefer the truth. Nuances. Context. Until December 2016, when I sought treatment in Arizona for insomnia, exhaustion, and self-medicating, I'd spent my entire life letting other people define who I was, feeling as if I had no voice in the matter. I'm through with that. Finally, it's my turn to bat. My turn to speak. My turn to dispel the accusations with honesty.

So, this is the story of a man in the mirror who, for most of a lifetime, would look in that mirror and see only a wounded little boy looking back at him. A story with the highest of highs and the lowest of lows. And a story wrapped in lessons that, I hope, will enlighten people who are ignorant about the subject of child sex abuse and will help those who have faced the kind of betrayal I have.

If they're like me, some of these people have paired lives of public success with private misery, trying to live in the "now" but forever dogged by the "then." Others have been swept away in a tsunami of addictions, broken relationships, and failure to hold a job. Still others, unable to reconcile with the hurts of the past, have killed themselves.

For those who remain, the irony is that what ultimately frees us is our willingness to stand up and bear witness to what happened to us— perhaps to family and trusted friends, to the police, to a therapist, and maybe—as I'm doing here—to the public at large. We finally share what our betrayers hoped we would take to our graves, because our silence allows them to continue to prey on those afraid to speak up.

One by one, as if bombing victims in a war not of our making, we wander out of the smoke and rubble, daring to tell our stories.

This is mine.

Chapter 1

May 1973. It's the bottom of the ninth inning and Los Angeles is down 4-3 to Philadelphia at Dodger Stadium. Davey Lopes, the Dodgers' second baseman, is on second base after a double off the left-center wall. Clean-up hitter Bill Russell, the potential winning run, is at the plate. But there are two outs. It's do-or-die time.

In the press box, radio broadcaster Vin Scully leans toward the microphone. *"Two-and-two to Russell. Carlton delivers. Swing and a high drive to deep left field! Back goes Luzinski to the warning track ... to the—"*

"Jimmy, time for dinner!" yells Mom from the kitchen.

"... wall. She is gone! The Dodgers win on a two-run homer by Bill Russell in the bottom of the ninth!"

"Honey, did you hear me?" she says, leaning out the sliding-glass door. "Dinner!"

"Comin', Mom."

WHEN I WAS a kid growing up in Pinole, California, the one-boy games that I'd play on the north side of our house on Diablo Court were, to me, as real as the ones Scully himself described at Chavez Ravine. I wasn't just hitting a plastic ball with a plastic bat; no, that would be to misunderstand the power of the mind. I was creating my own games. I was digging into batter's boxes in stadiums from LA to New York. More specifically, I was escaping into my imagination to run from a reality I didn't want to face.

Initially, Mom thought I was talking to myself a lot; no, I *was* manager Walter Alston doing a post-game interview. I *was* the entire Dodger team chattering away as we beat the Giants 4-3 in the bottom of the fifteenth. I *was* Lopes, Russel, Jimmy Wynn—whoever I wanted to be. That imaginary stadium was my favorite place in the world.

MY LEAST FAVORITE was the rectory at St. Joseph Catholic Church. But, first, an introduction to the place I called home. Pinole, California, straddles Interstate 80 about fifteen miles north of Berkeley, on San Pablo Bay. I was born in Stockton but moved to Pinole in first grade. The town offered a touch of Mayberry—Blackie's Hamburgers and Antler's Tavern were legendary—and a jolt of sprawling suburbia. Pinole was like a lot of Northern California towns in the 1970s, not particularly distinctive but, despite a few rough edges, pleasant enough.

We were close enough to San Francisco-Oakland for our parents to commute to big-time jobs—the new Bay Area Rapid Transit System (BART) started phasing in when I was a child—and for folks to take in pro sports events in the cities. Equally nice, we were far enough from the Pacific Ocean so we weren't shrouded in fog. Our temperatures were ten to fifteen degrees warmer than places on San Francisco Bay, our skies often blue, our winds often only tickling the palm trees sprinkled across town or the golden grass covering the hills beyond us.

I had one of the major leagues' first domed stadiums; on the rare occasions when it rained, my baseball games were moved into the garage.

Our window-less garage door—no automatic opener—had three horizontal rows of four panels each. After a one-hop bounce of the ball, I would bat my ball at the garage door and advance around the bases depending on which one I hit: a single for the bottom panels, a double for the middle panels, and a triple or home run for the upper panels.

During basketball season, every floor lamp in our house became a "hoop" through which I would shoot a pair of balled-up socks. Not particularly big for my age, I loved Nate "Tiny" Archibald, the former Texas-El Paso star who was drafted by the Cincinnati Royals in 1970 and became the only NBA player to lead the league in points and assists in the same season. Like me, he always looked younger than he actually was. When Archibald began in the NBA, in fact, the Celtics' Bob Cousy saw him in a hotel and thought he was a bellhop.

I loved being part of a team and knowing I contributed to its success; in some ways, I suppose my early life was a little like that of the narrator in the wonderful movie *The Sandlot,* where a kid yearning to belong finds his place in the world. Beyond sports, I loved fishing with my father, my grandpa and my Uncle Dan and their pals at Convict Lake near Mammoth Lakes; if everyone in the boat was catching fish, and I was contributing to our totals, that was pure, unadulterated bliss.

OUR FAMILY WAS nominally Lutheran, but I was an altar boy at St. Joseph Catholic Church. If that doesn't make sense, a lot about my story doesn't make sense. I had a friend, Robbie, who went to the church and Father Steve, a new associate priest at St. Joseph, invited me to join Robbie as an altar boy. It seemed like a good idea at the time. Why not?

I attended Ellerhorst Elementary School. Once, I saw a second-grade classmate of mine hanging from the back of his jeans on a flagpole cleat and helped him down. He'd been hung there like a coat by bullies who thought it was funny. His name was Morton, and he didn't have any friends. Except me.

For the first few weeks of school, I'd watched Morton emerge as the kid everyone liked to *not* like. First, it was casual neglect, then a few barbed comments, then what happened that Friday just before Halloween: I came into the courtyard and there he was, hanging on a cleat the janitor used to tie off the American and California flags. Morton was too ashamed to cry out; instead, he whimpered like a wounded animal. I helped him down. From that moment on I made a silent vow to myself: I'd have Morton's back.

It's not as if I was some big-for-his-age kid with a father who taught jujitsu and a mother who ran marathons; my father, Jim, was in the mortgage title business and my mother, Mary Jane, was a stay-at-home mom. I was small for my age and, though I loved boxing on ABC's *Wide World of Sports*, I can't remember ever being in a fight. Some would call me a goody two shoes. I'd call myself a guy who stood up for the underdog, and yet sometimes got bullied himself.

For as long as I can remember, people—particularly my Mom—called me a "pleaser." A peacekeeper. A fixer. A caregiver. At any rate, I befriended Morton. I once hung out with him all day long. I sat by him at lunch. We messed around after school. The works. It was no big deal. But it apparently was to him. Because a few days later the phone rang. It was his mother.

"Mrs. Bartko," his mother said to Mom, "what Jimmy did for Morton the other day was incredible. He can't stop talking about it. Nobody's ever treated him that way. That *nice*."

The way my mom conveyed the compliment to me, you'd have thought I'd brokered a peace deal between warring countries. But sure, it felt good to make someone's day. We never became best buds, Morton and I; in fact, I soon moved away. But I've never forgotten the thumbs-up I'd gotten from Morton's mom: if you're nice to people, I learned, you can, if even in a small way, change the world. Or at least someone's world.

But here's the problem with pleasers: We get so busy taking care of other people's needs that we sometimes forget about our own. Another thing about pleasers: What you see isn't always what you get. Here's what everybody saw when they looked at me when I was growing up: a happy-go-lucky kid living a sort of *Wonder Years* life; first house on your left as you turned into Diablo Court. Here's what they didn't see: a kid wearing a mask. A kid with a secret that nobody else could know, a secret that cloaked his private world in darkness. In pain. In uncertainty.

People like me are good at living in imaginary worlds that look, to the outsiders, like the epitome of innocence. In reality? It's the only way we know how to survive.

AT AGE EIGHT, I was the youngest player on our Lloyds Bank baseball team. Second base. I loved all sports, especially baseball. Hot dogs. Pretending I was Davey Lopes. And having my father as our head coach in the early years. I remember one game in particular: bottom of the last inning against Sportsman's, the league leaders, a team we hadn't beaten in five years. We needed one more out to clinch a victory. My mindset was clear: *hit it to me, pal.*

He did. Right up the middle. For a right-hander like me, the only way I could make the play was to backhand the ball, stop on a dime, pivot, and fire to first with everything I had. That's exactly what I did. The ball smacked into the glove of our first baseman just before the base runner's spikes hit the bag.

"Out!" yelled the ump.

Mitts and ball caps colored the California sky as my teammates celebrated. Me? I instinctively searched out my father in the dugout. His eyes said it all: wide, wonderful, locked on me. He bent down with his hands on my shoulders and shook his head as if part of him were incredulous and part of him expected nothing less of me.

"I … am … so … proud … of … you!" he said.

As I remember it, the words seemingly came out in slow motion, as if each was a stamp of approval. A kid doesn't forget words like that. When you're affirmed like that by an adult, it gives you the confidence to take on the world. But in the innocence of youth, I was about to encounter another "father" whose exploitation would taint that confidence—even if I didn't realize it at the time.

I CAME OF age in a relatively safe time in America—I was too young to serve in Vietnam, too naive to understand Watergate, too wrapped up in sports to give a lick about doing drugs. Beyond my personal world, life beyond spun wildly: I was four when Neil Armstrong walked on the moon in 1969, ten at the fall of Saigon in 1975, and fifteen when fifty-two American hostages in Iran were released in 1981.

My life orbited around two constants: family and sports, the former grounding me with a sense of security and the latter allowing my imagination to run wild. As much as I enjoyed friends, teams, and even school, I could be perfectly content alone. On Saturday mornings I watched the Major League game of the week on our 25-inch Magnavox—all nine innings. All by myself. No matter which two teams were playing.

And I loved boxing, an interest that came from my dad, who had done some sparring in the Marines. I was a huge George Foreman fan. I still remember the little ticker below some show reporting that my man had lost to Ali; I was lying on the floor while Mom and Dad were watching from the couch. I was crushed.

Unlike some of my buddies, who tussled with their parents, I loved my mom and dad—and still do. Dad was strict, sure, but not overly so. He was, however, something of a perfectionist, particularly when it came to the lawn; he'd mow it twice every Saturday. When it was my turn to do it, I'd get through the hard labor by pretending I was the Dodgers' groundskeeper, crisscrossing the design to make it look good for the upcoming game.

Dad worked for a title company, Ticor. My mom took care of me and my sister, Kim, who was two years older. She was your typical 1970s-'80s mom: making our meals, coming to my games, carting me around in the car, things I didn't appreciate at the time as much as I should have.

Dad taught me hard work, discipline, and how to field a grounder. Mom was the one who instilled in me the desire to care for others, like taking care of Morton. She tells of how I'd see some little old lady struggling to get across the street, and I'd go help her. She also brags about what a leader I was; not in a "my-way-or-the-highway" style, but in making up games in the backyard, at times involving my buddies, stuff like that. She says she can't remember me ever being in a fight. "You've always had a servant's heart," she says.

I know this will sound totally square, but my older sister, Kim, was among my best friends. We were far more amiable teammates than sibling rivals. And have remained so for our entire lives. I've always believed in her and she's always believed in me.

I was an above-average student, but not what you'd call a brain.

School came fairly easily for me but getting an "A" on a paper didn't stoke me like sinking a long shot in basketball or ripping a double in baseball. Or, for that matter, in simply being a well-rounded kid.

I wasn't an angel but honestly don't remember getting in any big-time trouble as a kid. For the most part, I did as I was told. That was the "pleaser" in me, an asset instilled, I suspect, by my mother and her mother, my grandma, Patricia. They were both sensitive, caring people—they embodied the phrase "unconditional love"—and I grew up thinking that's what I should offer the world, too. Be a giver, not a taker.

My biggest rebellion may have been when I was five. Mom wanted me to wear these black-and-white saddle shoes to kindergarten. *Are you kidding me?* I fought hard for tennis shoes—and won.

Once, in first grade, I did something wrong—can't even remember what it was—and Dad sent me upstairs to my room.

"And don't come down until you have a smile on your face," he said.

I later came down smiling and crying at the same time, as if I could *will* myself to be happy even though, deep inside, I was not.

"Dad," I said. "I can't smile *all* the time."

Looking back, it's an apt metaphor for what would become my life. Until I was seven, I'd floated along as if on an inner tube on a meandering stream. But though I never heard them coming, the rapids were fast approaching. And they were followed by the terror of a waterfall I never could have imagined.

Chapter 2

Everybody in Pinole loved Father Steve, including me. I never thought of him so much as a priest at St. Joseph Catholic Church, which he was. None of us kids did. To us he was just a great guy we loved to hang out with, a larger-than-life ball of fun.

In his mid-twenties, he was a combination of our Catholic Youth Organization basketball coach, Santa Claus, and a big brother. He was the guy who'd round up a bunch of us and take us to Oakland Raiders football games or Golden State Warriors basketball games, often inviting us for sleepovers at the church's rectory afterward.

As an associate pastor at St. Joseph, Father Steve quickly connected with families and their kids soon after his arrival at the church in 1972, the same year he was ordained at St. Francis De Sales in Oakland and the same year I turned seven. That was a testament to his charisma.

He was large, with a big laugh and a beard. Light-hearted. Jovial. Fun to be around. We all looked up to him, thinking we were lucky to be worthy of his friendship. And our parents all trusted him, not only because he was a man of God but because he coached us and invested lots of time in us. Ask my mother today and she'll tell you the same thing: Steve Kiesle—pronounced KEE-SLEE—was special and had a following among us kids so magnetic that people began calling him the Pied Piper. The kids worshipped him. The parents, my folks included, had him over for dinner. The community at large embraced him.

Not that he was perfect. In the St. Joseph School gym, he did something while coaching basketball that terrified me: one particular drill. We'd be scrimmaging and if you committed a turnover, he'd stop practice with the sharp blast of his whistle.

"OK," he'd say, "fire away!"

At that command, all the boys who hadn't committed a turnover would take basketballs and, as if part of a game of dodge ball, fire at the player who had. Sometimes I was that boy. I remember balls hitting me from all angles. It frightened me so much—it was utterly humiliating—that I told my mother about the drill.

"I don't want to practice anymore," I said. "I don't want to be on the team. I *hate* that drill."

My mom wasted little time in calling Father Steve and politely pointing out that this was not a good idea. It was disrespectful to the boys. And, in my case, terrifying.

"I totally understand," he said. "I'm so sorry, Mrs. Bartko. I didn't look at it from the boys' point of view. No more dodge ball drills. I get it."

And he stuck to his word. His turnaround earned back his respect in Mom's eyes and put me at ease.

At the time, I was a second-grader, a kid who, with the dodge-ball terror behind me, was living the dream. Raiders games. Warriors games. My imaginary games. Could life get any better?

It was not uncommon, after a trip into Oakland or San Francisco to watch a game with Father Steve, for us to stop at an all-you-can-eat restaurant called Harry's Hofbrau, next to the Oakland Coliseum on

Hegenberger Road. Our folks were happy to allow us to go on such trips, stuffing a little money in our hands for concession-stand treats and dinner.

Sometimes a handful of us spent the night at the rectory but usually just me and my pal, Robbie. It wasn't a matter of convenience; it's not as if the trip to Oakland or San Francisco was a long way and the rectory was part-way there. The trip was about twenty to twenty-five miles and the rectory was right in Pinole. Staying with Father Steve was just an extension of the day's fun: popcorn, movies, games. We loved it, especially when he'd tell us stories, usually some sports-oriented yarn of which we were inevitably the heroes.

One Friday, in the winter of 1973, it was just Robbie and me along on this particular overnighter. After the game and dinner, we arrived at the rectory, just to the left of the church, which sat on the corner of Plum Street and Tennant Avenue. The church was across the street from the fire station and just a few blocks from Antler's, a bar and grill dating to 1890 where my dad and the other coaches went to draft Little League baseball teams each year.

The rectory's front door opened into a fairly big open room that had a couple of couches. It was flanked to the right by a kitchen, and beyond that the lone bedroom and bathroom. Father Steve, as usual, offered us snacks while KTVU's sports news showed game highlights on the small television. It was always fun hearing about a game we'd just been to. It made us feel big-time, just like spending the night with our coach did.

About midnight it was time for bed. By now, we knew the routine. In Father Steve's bedroom, we'd get on our pajamas as Father Steve changed into his, taking off his clerical collar, of course, in the process. As usual, just before bed he'd offer us some wine and bread left over from church; it was cool to be on the "other side of Mass"—the ones receiving the elements, instead of the ones delivering "the goods," so to speak. It, too, made us feel important. Father Steve would always wipe the rim of the chalice with a handkerchief between offering us sips, just as he did at church.

A strange ritual for a priest and a couple of kids? Sure, but when you're seven, Mass is strange, too; the line between right and wrong isn't nearly as clear as it is when you're older. We drank the wine. *Yuck.* It tasted terrible; give me Kool-Aid any day. The wine made me feel a little light-headed. Father Steve would drink deeply himself, stroking his beard and licking his lips between sips.

Finally, he would, as we slipped into bed—Robbie always on the left side of him, me on the right—start telling us a bedtime story. In such stories, Robbie and I always hit the game-winning home run, sank the game-winning basket, and threw the game-winning pass.

Only this night was different. When the story was over, we didn't just go to sleep. Instead, Father Steve pulled me close to him. I thought he was just showing affection, like my dad might hug me. I was wrong. In a few moments, though I didn't realize it at the time, he was sexually abusing me for the first time. It would not be the last. In the nearly three years between early 1973 and late 1975, Father Steve Kiesle would sexually abuse me nearly three dozen times.

I'VE CHOSEN NOT to share the specific details of these encounters. It's extremely painful for me to conjure those images. And I don't believe the specifics should be necessary for a reader to understand what I went through. If someone has been in a terrible automobile accident, our empathy for the victim shouldn't be dependent on the wreck somehow being sufficiently grisly.

Horrible is horrible. From a distance of more than forty years, I see no ambiguity in the man forcing himself on me. What he did to me—and made me do to him—was cruel, greedy, and wrong.

But as a seven-year-old child in early 1973, I was clouded in confusion. The Communion setup imbued his actions with a sense of the sacred. At the same time, threats he made to us made it clear that we were to never tell anyone. There was a monster just outside his window, he told us, and our telling anyone would unleash it—on us. As a little boy, it isn't easy distinguishing the real monsters from the fake ones. And so the interactions became our "little secret." As children, Robbie and I never talked about what was happening with each other or with anyone else.

Though I never noticed the context at the time, Father Steve would sometimes set his trap long before he'd pounce. After serving at

Communion or Mass, he'd offer me a sip of the leftover wine. "We can finish it off later," he'd say, "in the rectory."

Usually, he prefaced the event with a favor—a game or pizza, for example, making us feel both special—and like maybe we owed him something in return. And by coupling the experience with the sacraments, candles lit, he suggested that experience was linked to the holiness of God Himself.

The interactions with him became such a routine part of my life that I didn't think twice when he invited me for another Warriors game, nor did I even grow tense. I enjoyed the games. Once at the rectory, however, I remember feeling a twinge of fear. And afterward, I'd be drowning in a despair I can't even describe. I'd crawl out of bed—I was on the side nearest the bedroom door—and go into the other room. I'd roll into a ball on a couch and cry, my face chafed from his beard. That couch in the rectory came to be my "safe spot." It wasn't a "happy place" like my imaginary baseball diamond back home, but at the rectory it was my go-to place to feel some semblance of safety, my refuge amid the roiling confusion. Our couch at home became my safe spot, too, when I couldn't sleep, which was often.

As the months, even years passed, the abuse continued. A few different lead-ins. A few different scenarios. But culminating in the same thing. In the morning, after a sleepover, he'd drop us off at our houses, give us high-fives, and act as if nothing had happened. But deep down, I never was fully at peace about the incidents. Why couldn't I sleep at night, thinking about the encounters? Why had my speech started to be sprinkled with a bit of a stammer?

I told nobody about Father Steve's involvement with me. I wasn't sure whether what he was doing was wrong. But I did sense that telling my parents would somehow disappoint them—and, warped as it might sound, might disappoint Father Steve. I was, after all, a kid who wanted to keep peace.

If I was fuzzy about what was happening to me, I was crystal clear about two things: Whatever was happening between Father Steve and me, it was all my fault; it had to be—because everyone loved the guy. And nobody else could ever know about it, especially my parents.

Two years after the nights in the rectory began, Father Steve was promoted and transferred to another community. Even then, he managed a few get-togethers with Robbie and me at his new rectory. But in 1977 my father got a new job in Modesto. At the end of my sixth-grade year, we moved. Kim, my sister, had only a year left of high school so she chose to stay and live with a friend in Pinole so she could graduate with the kids she'd gone to school with her whole life. Mom and Dad reluctantly allowed it.

Even though I don't remember any sort of official goodbye with Father Steve, it was refreshing to start anew. Sure, I missed some of my pals back in Pinole, notably Robbie, but I made new friends fast and soon was making the transition into my teenage years. And, of course, with Father Steve gone I no longer had the emotional burden of repeated instances of whatever it was that he had done to me.

Not, of course, that the dark nights, tears, and retreats to the family couch magically disappeared with the move. I seldom got a decent night of sleep after Father Steve first touched me. But distractions lessened the pain.

As the 1970s played out, it was a feel-good time for teenagers. Vans shoes. Video games. And, as the 1980s arrived, Valley Girls. Unlike the experience of my parents, there wasn't a depression or war to face. Unlike the experience of baby boomers, there wasn't the angst of Vietnam and cultural chaos.

We wore parachute pants, Members Only gear, and Converse All-Stars. Even though ours was a far more suburban than urban community, our schools had their share of boom boxes. But I was less into fashion trends than into football teams, basketball teams, and baseball teams. My dad and I became big Michigan football fans. Because his boss and his wife had gone to Michigan, we heard a lot about the Wolverines. And we soon became unlikely fans of Coach Bo Schembechler and the University of Michigan teams; I dreamed of someday watching a game in the 100,000-seat Big House in Ann Arbor.

In middle school I was smart enough to make our "Kids Bowl" team, sort of like *Who Wants to Be a Millionaire?* for brainy young teenagers, but I was out of my league. I had teammates who had memorized the dictionary. Me? I'd memorized the Dodgers' media guide, but not much beyond that. And, frankly, that didn't bother me a bit. I loved sports. To a kid who needed an escape, they were my daily retreat.

At night, my retreat was to the couch, my "safe spot."

"Jimmy, why won't you stay in your bed?" one of my parents would ask.

"Can't sleep. Just need to watch a little TV."

They tried to stop the routine, but over time I think they just realized it was easier to relent.

In 1978, the year I turned thirteen, I was at home eating lunch when our lemon-yellow wall phone rang. My mother answered.

"Oh, my God. He did *what*? I can't believe it."

Uh-oh. Was I toast?

She furtively glanced at me, then stretched the phone cord around the wall so she was in the dining room and I couldn't hear her. After hanging up, she looked at me with a deeply furrowed brow. *What had I done wrong?*

"Jimmy, that was a friend of mine from back in Pinole," she told me. "Father Steve has been arrested for, uh, 'inappropriate contact' with young boys. You remember him, don't you? He's the one who took you to ball games, your basketball coach."

"Sure, yeah, I remember him," I said while thinking *what in the world is "inappropriate contact?"* But I didn't want to remember him, even if I did—every day. Every night. My heart pounded, my mouth got dry.

"I need to ask you a very difficult question," Mom said. I looked away—to anywhere but at her eyes. "Did Father Steve ever—I mean when you were with him, was there ever a time when he, uh, made you feel uncomfortable? When he did something to you?"

"Something like what?"

"Touch you in any way that didn't seem appropriate."

For the first time since I'd met Father Steve I felt as if a connection had been made to what had happened, not that I understood what this all meant. Just that it must have been bad. For the first time I realized: *someone else might know.* Part of me wanted to blurt out "yes" so I would no longer have to be the lone Keeper of the Secret. But a bigger part of me didn't want the shame of disappointing her and Dad, of hurting Father Steve, of rippling any of the waters on the smooth surface of my life's lake.

"No, Mom," I said. "Never."

She looked hard at me, squinting her eyes a tad.

"You're sure, Jimmy?"

"I'm sure."

She nodded her head slowly but a touch more confidently, as if she really wanted to believe me.

"OK. I'm glad to hear that."

But she wasn't convinced I was telling the truth, because later that day she again asked if Father Steve had touched me inappropriately. And, again, I denied it. I remembered that Bible story about Peter having denied Christ three times. I was only one denial away from tying his lifetime record. And I realized: It's tough being put on the spot like that. I rationalized that to deny anything had happened wasn't an actual lie, just a withholding of the truth for the good of all involved. A white lie, which was OK, right?

But in time my denial backfired. I not only was burdened with the guilt and shame for having allowed Father Steve to touch me, but with the guilt and shame for having lied to the mother I loved and respected. I mentally kicked myself for not telling her the truth.

But I would repeatedly tell myself that worse than lying was disappointing her and Dad. I just couldn't do that.

Chapter 3

My high school years began in 1980 to the sounds of Def Leppard, Men at Work, Journey, and Brian Adams. MTV was born when I turned sixteen. Nintendo emerged as our generation's cool computer game. We'd get together, listen to tunes, play some cards, and head for Taco Bell at midnight; I'd have two or three bean burritos—no onions—and a small Pepsi. Mullet hairstyles were all the rage and, I confess, I had one, aptly defined as "business in the front, party in the back."

Midway through my teenager years, I first started to understand the context of what Father Steve had done to me. At Somerset Junior High, we had a sex-ed class. When our teacher explained "good touching from bad touching," I realized that the priest had violated me. That what Father Steve had done was terribly wrong.

I attended Central Catholic High in Modesto. Our family was Lutheran but my folks had no problem when, because of the influence of a Catholic girlfriend and pals of mine, I converted to Catholicism; I was confirmed into the church as a junior in high school. Strange, given what had happened to me, I realized. But the church hadn't abused me, one person had. Not, of course, that I planned to ever tell anyone about it.

Meanwhile, I emerged as a decent basketball and baseball player. A buddy, Roger Orth, and I had this whiffle ball league in his backyard, which we imagined to be Wrigley Field in Chicago. We were a team and we took on all comers. There were no bases to run, just all these places in the field that were designated as a homer, triple, double, single, or out. Roger was a lefty pitcher and had a riser that nobody could hit. I had a screwball that batters were equally baffled by. Together, Roger and I were unbeatable.

I was blessed with lots of friends. I was getting decent grades and having fun. Then, shortly before my junior year came news that blind-sided me: my father had again been transferred, this time to Spokane, Washington.

"Jimmy, what do you think?" said Mom. "Isn't that exciting?"

Mom and Dad eagerly eyed me. The move from Pinole to Modesto had been fairly easy, but this was different. I was a starter on various sports teams and tight with friends. I had a girlfriend. What's more, I didn't have an abuser who was making my life a quiet hell, someone I was more than happy to escape on the last move.

"I don't wanna go," I said. "You go. I'll stay and finish up my last two years here. I can live with Aunt Pat and Uncle Tom."

"But Jimmy, you can play on ball teams in Spo—"

"I *don't* want to go."

My folks didn't like the idea, my mother in particular. But after multiple go-rounds, I think they realized they'd have to pry me out of California with a crowbar. Reluctantly, they agreed to let me stay and live with my aunt and uncle for my last two years of high school.

My decision absolutely crushed my mother—she stayed in bed for four days mourning the temporary breakup of our family. In her eyes, she'd lost her son for good; after all, I would head for college after graduating from high school, never again to be a permanent part of their household. But peer pressure is a strong force when you're sixteen; in this case it was trumped by an otherwise natural tendency to please everyone.

At the time I couldn't see why Mom was so upset by my decision. But now I do. Becoming a sudden empty nester blindsided her. In retrospect, I realize that the kid who was loath to let those around him hurt was doing exactly that: inflicting pain on the ones he loved most. Following my refusal to come clean about the abuse, I now had two strikes against me for letting people down.

As my high school years rolled to an end, I was sad to be apart from my parents and, as always, sleeping on the couch most nights, racked with fear and guilt. But in the end, the decision not to follow my parents north worked out. Would I make the same choice again? Probably not. Would Mom and Dad have wanted me to make the same choice again? Probably not. But the two years went fast, and my folks and I maintained a strong, loving relationship, thanks, I suppose, to my parents' willingness to forgive my stubbornness.

By the time I graduated from high school in 1983—I hit .525 my senior year in baseball—my father in Spokane had become president of Washington State's Cougar Club. Pullman, home of WSU, was a seventy-five-minute drive from Spokane. And with the school not being a Pac-10 powerhouse, I thought there was a chance I could play on the baseball team and fulfill my dream of playing at the collegiate level.

But Jim Walden, the WSU football coach, and his assistant coach, Jimmy Burrow, knew a bit about me through knowing my father as the Cougar Club president. They made me an offer I couldn't refuse: a job as the WSU football manager.

Though it would become life changing once I made it, the decision was not an easy one. At the time, my girlfriend and I were in love—I didn't want to leave her. But we were also young and had aspirations that weren't meshing; we decided to part ways.

When I arrived at school I briefly worried that I might have made a mistake; every other manager had quit. Until I found some help, I was *it*—the lone manager. But as I brought on a guy to assist me, something wonderful happened: I realized that I was in my element here. This was a manifestation of what my mother had always said about me having a "servant's heart."

I charted plays from the sideline. I timed punts. I pretended I was an outside linebacker biting on the fake pitch from the quarterback to the tailback. I even drove the equipment truck, all of which made me grow up in a hurry. At some point I remember deciding, *I'm gonna take this seriously. I'm gonna be the best manager ever.*

Because I wasn't working beneath anybody else, I had no choice but to figure things out on my own. I learned to improvise. To think for myself. And I was forever getting in bizarre situations. I mentioned the equipment truck. I'd never driven any sort of a large truck. But there I was, with another manager in the passenger seat, driving a six-wheeler through ice and snow down the Columbia Gorge. We'd be headed to Corvallis or Eugene in Oregon, knowing that if we didn't get these helmets, shoulder pads, pants and jerseys to their destination, WSU would forfeit the game. That was big-time pressure. But my thought process was an extension of the same thought process that had driven me from the get-go: *Don't disappoint anyone.*

I was welcomed by the team and staff, never made to feel like I was a servant. Instead, the sense was: *Jimmy's just part of the team.* I loved it. In the years to come I traveled to an array of cool places: Columbus, Ohio, for a game against Ohio State; Knoxville for a game with Tennessee; the Rose Bowl in LA twice for games against UCLA; Memorial Coliseum in LA twice for games against USC; even to Tokyo, in 1987, for a game against California. (Nothing like traveling 10,000 miles roundtrip to tie a football game, 17-17.)

But by far the coolest experience was my freshman year, 1983, when we played—and nearly beat—Michigan in the Big House—my dream team and stadium. The Cougars fought hard before dropping a 20-17 game to a team that would finish eighth in The Associated Press final poll and play in the Sugar Bowl. The crowd was 103,256 people, more than four times what we averaged per game in Pullman's Martin Stadium.

Before the game, I walked into that stadium as if walking into a dream; it was my first game as a freshman manager. Our team's locker room doors opened right next to Michigan's—not the kind of setup you see anymore. Just as I left for the field, there, right next to me, was Michigan Coach Bo Schembechler, flanked by a few law-enforcement guys. As we walked next to each other, I didn't know if it violated pre-game protocol, but I couldn't help myself.

"Coach, hey, I'm Jimmy Bartko—Washington State's head manager. I'm obviously rooting for my Cougs today, but I've been a fan of you and Michigan most of my life."

He draped an arm around my shoulder.

"Well, now, how does a kid out in Pullman, Washington, become a Michigan fan?"

I told him about how my dad's boss and his wife had gone to Michigan; how their love for the Wolverines had become our love for the team, too. Once we were out on the field and tending to our respective teams, our team photographer, knowing my fondness for Bo, snapped a great non-staged photo of the two of us walking almost stride for stride with each other. I later mailed a print to Coach Schembechler.

"Great meeting you, Mr. Schembechler," I wrote. "Would you mind autographing this and returning it?" Weeks later he did so, writing "Good luck with the Cougs, Jimmy—Bo Schembechler." I framed it and put it on my fraternity-room wall.

I LEARNED MORE in four years of managing the WSU football team than I did in any classroom. We had three people doing the job that schools today would have at least a dozen people doing, each of us working about fifty hours per week. We'd load trucks and airplanes for road games. Roll all the new footballs over our hotel rugs the night before an away game to make sure the sheen was off them and they could be gripped better. Arrange with restaurants for post-game meals for seventy-five guys. Drive game film to Spokane right after a game so it could get flown to whoever we played the next week—and pick up theirs. Sometimes we'd get requests that were tough to fulfill.

"Jimmy, we need a half-case of beer," some coach would say. "Bud Light."

"But coach, I'm only eighteen."

"Figure it out, Jimmy. Do what you have to do."

Gradually, I did. I gained confidence. I drove a red Chevy LUV pickup that my parents had given to me. I joined a highly respected fraternity, Alpha Tau Omega. I learned to do all the hard work behind the scene so things would be easier for the team. Really, these were among the best years of my life.

At Memorial Coliseum in LA in 1985, we had a student manager, Greg, who had some physical challenges. A few members of the USC band noticed that he was struggling to pick up multiple footballs off the turf; just as he would have the last one in the bag, some band member would stick out a foot, or bump him, and knock Greg down. And, again and again, the balls would be rolling around so Greg would have to start over.

The next year, before USC came to Pullman for a game, there was talk of payback. Mark Rypien, a future Super Bowl MVP but then a senior for WSU, and Ken Woody, an assistant coach, hatched an idea. In warm-ups, they sent WSU wide receivers on sideline patterns, whereupon Rypien "accidentally" overthrew three or four receivers. The footballs hit band members as if scud missiles. I loved it. We all did. And it was way better—and less apt to get me thrown in jail—than another coach's idea: have me sneak into the band's dressing room and put itching powder in their uniforms.

I'll never forget an old high school pal calling me once to see how I was doing out there on the Palouse, a happy island of college kids surrounded by miles of wheat fields.

"What can I say? I'm living the dream!"

My senior year I lived with Butkus, a Golden Shepherd mix, and a bunch of football players, including one, Dan Weber, who had an eight-foot boa constrictor. I hated snakes and told Dan as much. I should point out that Dan was a 6'7" defensive lineman who weighed 290 pounds. I was 5'7" and weighed about 140 pounds. But I held my ground. "If I find that snake out of its tank even one time, I'll cut it in half." I never had a problem with the snake, not because of my threat but because Dan was a big teddy bear who understood.

I can't think of much I didn't do involving WSU's athletic department. I sold hot dogs and popcorn. I worked with different athletic teams, including a basketball team that started a game against Arizona at WSU's Friel Court and, because of a power outage, finished it at nearby

Bohler Gym. I kept statistics at Autzen Stadium in Eugene for the Cougars on the day in 1984 when WSU's Rueben Mayes set the NCAA single-game rushing record with 357 yards against Oregon. (I could have driven the team's equipment truck through some of those holes.) I did promotion, marketing, you name it.

I committed so much time to that team that, along with my studies, my mind had little time to wander to the past. To the rectory. To the abuse. And that was just fine. Sports were fun, safe, and well-defined. Every field was 100 yards long, every football regulation size, every quarter 15 minutes in length. But the past was dark, confusing, and uncontained, the abuse like the stench of some putrid Pandora's Box, though only I knew it existed. So, I pretended it had never happened.

Ultimately, after graduation, I became the assistant director of marketing—basically the job I was already doing, but for higher pay. I'd leave the Palouse within six months, but I had one more lesson to learn before moving on, and it wasn't an easy one. I learned that good intentions aren't always enough when it comes to seeing the people around you hurt.

IN 1988, WHEN I was twenty-three, Cougar boosters had played a golf tournament in Walla Walla, and coaches and the athletic staff were having a few beers on the way home later that night. I was with the new WSU head football coach, Dennis Erickson, and two associate athletic directors, Bill Moos, and Lynn Rosenbach, whose son Timm was a star quarterback at WSU. Timm was a great friend of mine and Lynn someone I respected deeply.

Lynn, fifty-three, wasn't in the best of health, having already lost an arm to cancer. Suddenly, he started bleeding from the mouth; a tumor had burst, we later learned. We didn't have time to wait for an ambulance; we were a good ninety minutes from Spokane and forty-five minutes from Colfax, which had a small hospital.

"Jimmy, quick, get in the car," said Moos, who'd lost an eye in a hunting accident and didn't like driving at night. "We're taking him to Colfax. Dennis needs to take care of Lynn in back. You drive!"

The day had grown dark and windy. This was before cell phones, so it's not like we could call his wife, "Rosie," or Timm. We got him in the car. He started blacking out. I drove like the proverbial bat out of hell. Once in Colfax, before we could get him medical attention, Erickson and I gave him CPR for agonizing minutes—with no results.

"Come on, come on, Lynn, you got this!" I said.

"Wake up, Lynn," said Erickson. "Don't give up on us!"

But he died right there, on our watch. On *my* watch. And, in a sense, I felt as if I'd failed him. As if I were to blame.

At twenty-two, I stood there with the blood of a dead man—a friend, a mentor—on my hands, having learned that no matter how badly you wanted to help someone, sometimes they couldn't be helped.

I never stopped to think that, in some ways, like Lynn, I needed help myself, even if my pain wasn't anything like his. I hid it well under a veneer of on-the-go activity. Lynn's pain was physical, there for all to see, whether he wanted anyone to see it or not. Mine was quiet, hidden, whether I wanted to keep enduring it or not. And even if I had the guts to ask for help, I made sure there was no time for it. I busied myself taking care of everyone around me, making sure that whether it was a football uniform, publicity, or CPR, the people around me all had what they needed to sustain them. That was my job. Help others get what they needed.

There was no time for me and whatever wounds I had. And with what little free time I did have I spent convincing myself of this: that I wasn't actually wounded. Like my childhood baseball games, in which whatever I wished could happen did happen, maybe I could make whatever did happen *not* happen.

Maybe.

Chapter 4

While I was transitioning from boy to man in the 1980s, Father Steve was sexually abusing more children. That's not unusual; studies show regressive pedophiles can abuse hundreds of youngsters in a lifetime. Father Steve's number, it would turn out, would be in triple digits.

Despite being arrested in 1978 in connection with the molestation of six children—it might have been seven, but, regrettably, I had stayed silent—Father Steve served no time and, in fact, continued to abuse victim after victim, boys and girls mainly in their elementary-school years and early teens. He would molest more than 200 children in his lifetime, according to Rick Simons, a Hayward, California, attorney who would represent two Kiesle victims who sued the priest. (See p. 230 for complete Kiesle timeline.)

"Of all the priests I've met who abused children—and there's probably a couple dozen—he was by far the most evil, remorseless socio-path of the lot," said Simons.

Two things allow such predators to continue doing what they're doing for so long: First, their ability to convince people, even victims, that they're wonderful human beings who aren't doing something bad. And, second, their good fortune—and their victims' bad fortune—to have people around them who cover for them. Secrecy is the glue that binds the priests together; they watch out for each other. And when the priests are caught, the church's hierarchy acts like a street cop simply tell-ing someone to "move along. Find some other place."

And they do. Bishops reassign molesting priests to new parishes, where—surprise—they find new victims. The bishops sometimes ignore the abuse because they, too, are molesting children. The Catho-lic Church recycles child sex abusers; it's a long tradition. And Kiesle is among those it recycled.

As early as 1968, four years before I would first be victimized by him, Kiesle began what would be a quarter-century of abusing children. At the time he was a seminary student at St. Patrick's in Menlo Park, Cal-ifornia, near Stanford University, having been drawn to the priesthood by his mother, a devout Catholic. In 1969 he abused a boy and shortly thereafter a girl. But his "official" reputation within the school was a let-ter on file lauding him as a young man who had "excellent rapport with teenagers."

Despite some faculty members finding Kiesle hard-headed and dif-ficult to get along with, he was nevertheless ordained in 1971 as a sub-deacon by the Diocese of Oakland and was assigned to be deacon to Rev. Louis Dabovich at Church of the Good Shepherd in Pittsburg, California.

Dabovich saw red flags, though apparently not involving sexual abuse. In 1972, Bishop Floyd Begin wrote that Dabovich was "deeply concerned" about Kiesle. Dabovich said Kiesle could be "immature and difficult to communicate with … ." Only two months later, however, Kiesle petitioned to advance to the order of the priesthood and, in May 1972, he was ordained by the Diocese of Oakland.

So, whatever concerns the two men had, those concerns obviously weren't enough for them to withhold their stamp of approval regarding Kiesle and the priesthood—or they were deeply concerned but rationalized that reassignment was a solution. (A solution for *them*, of course, not for the potential victims and their families in the new area of the priest's reassignment.)

In the fall of 1972, soon after Kiesle arrived in Pinole, his evaluation by the diocese noted he got along with children "exceptionally well." But the next year he sexually abused me, Robbie, and, presumably, others who have never gone public.

That Kiesle became known as "the Pied Piper" in Pinole took on a sick irony when it was learned just where the "six-foot-tall teddy bear," as one resident described him, was leading these children. For the next six years, as he bounced from our church to another to another in the Bay Area, one thing remained constant: his molestation of children. Dozens and dozens of them.

Finally, in 1978, the law caught up with him. That summer, police showed up at Our Lady of the Rosary Church in Union City, California, with a warrant for his arrest. Six boys had come forward, saying they had been molested by Kiesle while the senior pastor, Father George Crespin, was on sabbatical, according to the *Los Angeles Times.*

"A parent of one of the boys worked for the Alameda County Sheriff's Department and went to the authorities with the children's statements," the paper reported.

Kiesle was charged in connection with the tying up and sexual abuse of two boys. Crespin noted something odd about Kiesle's reaction during the arrest. He seemed relieved, the *Los Angeles Times* reported in an April 18, 2010, article by Victoria Kim. "As if he had been waiting for this day to come," she wrote.

He surrendered to authorities and eventually pleaded no contest to criminal charges of molesting children. He took a leave of absence, attended counseling, and reported regularly to a probation officer. That, on top of a three-year probation, allowed him to have his record wiped clean.

Two years later—about the time my folks moved to Spokane and I chose to finish high school in Modesto—Kiesle asked to be defrocked—stripped of his priestly privileges and functions. His reason, he wrote, was that he had a "potential wife."

(She would, it turned out, become his wife after he left the priesthood. She was the mother of my friend, Robbie, who was usually abused while I was being abused, though his mother wouldn't know this for decades. When Kiesle was arrested, Robbie's mother, like mine, asked if he'd been among the boys the man had molested. Like me, he denied it, later telling me the "shame and guilt" wouldn't allow him to speak up.)

Father Crespin assumed Kiesle's defrocking would take only a rubber stamp from the Vatican; after all, the Diocese of Oakland was united in making the recommendation. Why would anyone fight for Kiesle's right to stay?

But here's where a strange and sickening story grew stranger and sicker. The Kiesle case started spinning in an eddy of red tape and lethargy whose underlying message was this: the Vatican was reluctant to part with the priest. As early as 1981 John S. Cummins, bishop of Oakland, urged the Vatican to cut ties with Kiesle. In February 1982 Cummins wrote, "It is my conviction that there would be no scandal if this petition were granted and that ... given the nature of the case, there might be greater scandal to the community if Father Kiesle were allowed to return to active ministry."

In response, the Vatican reacted with a collective yawn. Among its unstated, but obvious, reasons? A shortage of priests. In a 1985 letter made public in 2010, the *Los Angeles Times* reported that Cardinal Joseph Ratzinger, at the time the Vatican's chief enforcer of doctrine, wasn't inclined to defrock Kiesle. So many priests were abandoning the priesthood that Ratzinger, in a letter, suggested parting ways with Kiesle did not seem to be for the "good of the Universal Church." (See p. 229 for the complete letter.)

This wasn't some priest who someone said was "too friendly" with kids; this was a priest who'd been convicted by law of sexually abusing children. Ratzinger noted that the case was of "grave significance" but pointed to "the detriment that [defrocking] can provoke within the community of Christ's faithful" and said the Vatican needed more time to consider Kiesle's request.

It's mindboggling that Ratzinger's reluctance to defrock Kiesle overlooks the most important thing here: the victims, myself among them. That a man of his spiritual stature—he would later be handsomely promoted—couldn't, or wouldn't, muster the courage to defend "the least of these" is beyond comprehension. What's more, it's pathetic that Cummins, the bishop, based his "defrock-him" argument *not* on the fact that the man been found guilty of abusing children, but on the premise that letting him stay might create a "greater scandal in the community." In other words, what really mattered wasn't the children and their families, but the reputation of the church.

Father Crespin saw the decision as something of a "friendly divorce" or as he called it, "a slam dunk." And yet it would take another two years before the Vatican finally relented and defrocked Kiesle, meaning that from the time he pled guilty to the time he was let go took six years.

It gets worse. In 1985, while the diocese was trying to have Kiesle defrocked, a pastor in Pinole allowed the man to volunteer at his church— my old church, St. Joseph—for years. Where within the church? In the *youth* department. The Diocese of Oakland later took no responsibility, saying it was unaware that Kiesle was volunteering, according to Maurine Behrend, an Office of Youth Ministry leader within the diocese.

Why not? Shouldn't the pastor of the church who welcomed him have done even a cursory background check that would have shown that only seven years earlier Kiesle had been convicted of child molestation?

Instead, it was Behrend who blew the whistle. She first encountered Kiesle on Youth Day in April 1988, subsequently learning from another minister that the priest had been convicted of molestation. She alerted the head of the youth ministry office and personally warned Cummins, the bishop of Oakland, who, years before, had supported Kiesle's defrocking. She also sent a letter of outrage to a church official, demanding to know why "a convicted child molester is currently the youth ministry coordinator at St. Joseph Parish in Pinole."

"The fact was reported to you in September when Steve's name was turned in as coordinator," wrote Behrend. "It was reported again in January when people from St. Anne's in Union City recognized Steve at Youth Day (and were furious), I reported it to Sister Leonard on April

13 after Steve requested to be part of the preparations for [a youth rally], and I mentioned it to the bishop on April 29 … How are we supposed to have confidence in the system, when nothing is done?"

This is how the Catholic Church often deals with priests who've been caught molesting kids: it reassigns them to other churches in hopes that their pasts won't follow them. Never mind that the victims' pasts *always* follow *them*.

Decades later, when I learned of all this, I was glad to see someone—Behrend—finally had the decency, the courage, and the compassion to say: *What is going on here? This isn't right. This isn't acceptable.* But within the Catholic system, such whistle-blowers are the exception, not the rule, writes Jason Berry in *Lead Us Not into Temptation.* Letters come to the church by the hundreds with accusations about abuse, but little is done in response.

Kiesle wasn't removed until Cummins bumped into the priest—in another sick irony—at a child's confirmation ceremony. The next day Cummins made it clear that Kiesle wasn't to be found on any parish grounds in the diocese, as a volunteer or otherwise.

At times, perpetrators and their defenders prosper while victims are forgotten. After I'd grown up, after I would finally go public with the revelation that I was abused as a child, I would be forced out as athletic director at a Division I university. But Cardinal Joseph Ratzinger, the man who stalled in defrocking the priest who abused me, would get a prestigious promotion. In 2005, he would be named head of the worldwide Catholic Church.

He would be known as Pope Benedict XVI.

Chapter 5

It was 1988. Now in my early twenties, I dragged my childhood into adulthood like a ball and chain. The solution of forgetting the past was to stay busy in the present. I took a job as the head of University of Oregon's Duck Athletic Fund for Southern Oregon/Northern California. Basically, I was a fundraiser.

I'd gotten the job in the fall of 1988 because of a connection at WSU. Kim Schwartz—a Kappa Kappa Gamma at WSU whose father, Mike, was a big University of Oregon donor in Eugene and whose godfather was Rich Brooks, the Ducks' football coach—told me there was an opening at the UO for a regional fundraising director. I was interested but initially fearful about applying. But Kim kept encouraging me, and said she'd put in a good word for me. I finally applied and, after being interviewed by the guy I'd replace if I got the job, Mike Jorgensen, I was hired.

I started in January 1989, the year Oregon football rose from the depths of mediocrity.

I lived alone—with my dog Butkus—in a Medford apartment and threw myself into the job. I organized trips north and south for our supporters to watch UO football and basketball games in Eugene and in the Bay Area. Organized monthly luncheons where Duck fans could hear from our coaches, if even on a speaker phone. Joined Rogue Valley Country Club so I'd have easy access to a lot of the Duck alums and other supporters. Traveled a lot between San Francisco and Grants Pass. Made lots of friends. At twenty-four, I felt as if I was a surrogate son to a lot of these folks. I was invited to join families for Easter dinner, partied with people at Duck events, and played a lot of three-hole rounds of golf at Rogue Valley followed by happy hours that often went into overtime.

Not that every event went as planned. In the last week of October 1990, Brooks, the UO coach, was addressing our Duck Club at a Chinese restaurant in Medford by speaker phone in Eugene when those of us in the room heard a *pop, pop, pop* from outside.

"What was that?" Brooks asked.

"Not sure," I said. "We'll call you back."

I thought it was some sort of Halloween prank. Wrong. A bank had been robbed. The robber had been surrounded at our back door, shot, and killed—right next to my car in the parking lot. The thing I remember most was that as the police ushered the group of seventy-five attendees to the back of the kitchen for safety reasons, the chefs cooking our food never missed a beat. They kept mixing their stir-fry lunch amid the chaos, as if there weren't cops with rifles and panicky people everywhere around them.

I could relate; *never let 'em see you sweat.* The show must go on—just like my life after Pinole in the '70s. Live the lie. I did so, the abuse now fifteen years behind me. My friend, Robbie, I later learned, had "lived the lie" too. But in college, he told an aunt about Kiesle, now his stepfather, having abused him. He did so because he feared that her son—Robbie's cousin—might be at risk around Kiesle. As it turned out, the boy was spared. Only later would Robbie's aunt learn that although Kiesle had not abused her son, he'd molested her daughter.

For a sparsely populated place, Southern Oregon backed the Ducks well; we had more than a thousand season-ticket holders from that area. My job was made easier by the Oregon football team, in 1989, going to a bowl game for the first time since I'd been born. The Independence Bowl in Shreveport, Louisiana, might not have been the Granddaddy of Them All—I still haven't thawed out from that icy wind that blew through the open bleachers—but history suggests it was the beginning of a revitalization of Oregon football.

Much of what I learned in those two years in Medford regarding developing and maintaining a fan base were lessons I'd lean on for decades to come. Among them: show respect for people. Treat everyone the same. Whether someone donates millions or gives $100, make them feel special. (I'd hear this from time to time: *Jimmy, you're the only guy who returns my calls*). Don't be afraid to ask questions. Humbling yourself isn't a defeat, it's a victory, because people with the answers will help you do your job better.

One of my favorite lines in those two years was, "Hey, I'm new around here. Can you help me out?" I've always been suspicious of people who act as if they have all the answers. And, finally, never be afraid to try something new. It's a lesson that meshed nicely with what, in the late 1990s, would become Oregon's default format for doing business in the athletic department—and re-branding itself in the process.

My fundraising philosophy has always been about building relationships. When you meet someone, the first thing on his or her mind might not be a desire to part with $50,000. But if you build a relationship and earn people's trust—and that relationship is genuine, not just a means to an end—they'll be a whole lot more likely to listen and help if you share a need with them. They might also become a friend for life.

Harold Taylor was such a man. I met him soon after being elevated to the Portland region of the Duck Athletic Fund in 1991. Then in his eighties, he had founded Taylor Electric in Portland, and, in his retirement, helped revive Duck athletics with their first-ever seven-digit gift—$1 million. His huge donation set the tone for many others that followed.

Because of that unselfishness, I was always happy to help Harold out anyway I could. In 1995, at the Oregon-Illinois football game in

Champaign, I was sitting with him in the athletic directors box when he suddenly started clutching his chest.

"Harold, you OK? Do I need to call 911?"

"No, just need my nitro pills, Jimmy."

"Where are they?"

He checked his pockets. "I think I left them in the bus."

I raced down the steps—no time to wait for the elevator—and sprinted to the parking lot. When I got to the bus, the driver was gone. Somewhere in my past, I heard the voice of that WSU assistant coach who needed a six-pack: *Figure it out. Do what you've gotta do.* I ran to the ticket office, learned where the bus drivers were sitting at the game, found our driver, got him to open the bus, grabbed the pills, and raced back.

"Thanks, Jimmy," says Harold. "Mighta saved my life!"

Harold hadn't attended UO but I'll never forget how excited he was when I drove him to Eugene so he could present that $1 million gift that helped put the UO over the top in raising money for the Casanova Center, a new athletic-department headquarters, and new sky suites for Autzen Stadium. Harold taught me that you could be hugely successful financially and still be unselfish. As they say, "With wealth, a selfish person becomes more selfish and a generous person becomes more generous."

I met two other significant people in my life in the early 1990s: Eileen Sorensen and Phil Knight. Eileen worked for the Oregon Sports Network at UO. We hit it off in 1991 when she came to Medford as part of a donor event. She was smart, pretty, athletic, tough, and independent. Our first date was a Whitney Houston concert in Portland, for which I drove three hours to Eugene, picked her up, drove two hours to the concert, then reversed the northbound trip, arriving home in Medford in the wee hours. But she was worth it.

Nights, driving alone like that, were horrible. I could go months without being haunted by the past, then, bam, it would hit me. Nights in general were bad but a lot of situations made them worse. Any kind of anxiety at night was a recipe for bad memories. Not that nights were a prerequisite. Stepping into a Catholic church, which I continued to do, was bad. So, I ran from the bad stuff by trying to do good: work harder, raise more money, please my bosses—whatever it took to keep my mind off the memories I couldn't shake.

In 1991 I was transferred to Portland to do fundraising for the Ducks there and Eileen left UO to be a sales rep for Hinman Vineyards outside Eugene. The more we got to know each other, the more we decided this relationship had a future. That "more," of course, had an asterisk beside it when it came to me sharing about my past. If I'd told her about Father Steve, my pain would become her pain. What's more, she might consider me "damaged goods." I couldn't risk losing her, so I didn't tell her. Three years after we met, we were wed May 21,1994. Soon thereafter I was asked to join the "mother ship" in Eugene as an associate athletic director.

A few years earlier, at the Nike headquarters in Beaverton, I'd met Phil Knight at a "Ducks Night Out: A Tribute to Bill Bowerman" event I helped organize to honor the venerable UO track and field coach. While we were putting the finishing touches on the set-up that afternoon, Phil and his wife Penny had dropped by. I'd never met them. It was one of those aha moments where you're reminded that part of you is suddenly in the inner circle of a grown-up world and part of you is still a kid at a Golden State Warriors games seeking an autograph from one of your heroes.

Phil was relaxed and affable. I was nervous and trying to act like the wily veteran I was not. I was twenty-five years old. He seemed genuinely glad to meet me. I know I was thrilled to meet him. That night, I got a lesson in the respect people have for the man. Until then, I'd never seen anyone "take over a room" the way he had. Not in an obnoxious, over-bearing, ego-driven way, but in a "we're-all-part-of-the-Oregon-family" way.

Meanwhile, the respect he showed for Bowerman, who'd helped him launch Nike, was as deep as it was real. The evening was a four-hour "teachable moment" for me regarding the man. Before then I didn't know much about him beyond the fact that he was the Nike co-founder and among the wealthiest human beings in the world. What I realized that night is that he is so much more. He has a true passion to give to others, but only does so in partnership with his wife, Penny. He has a deep respect for people. And I sensed he has, like us all, a genuine need to *belong*—to be part of something greater than himself, the kind of thing sports can foster.

At the time, neither of us knew that we would become close partners in helping a good university become a great university—and close friends, to boot. All I knew was that I admired him deeply. As we worked together and traveled to away games in years to come, I gradually realized that the pauper-in-the-king's-court imbalance between us was melting like spring snow. Not because I started to think I was some sort of VIP but because Phil began paying me the kind of respect that I wondered if I deserved. Outwardly, I came across as confident, decisive, strong. Inwardly, none of the above. I'd lie awake nights, feeling shame for having let it happen to me, guilt for having told nobody, and weak for not being able to "get over it."

The best lesson Phil Knight would teach me was to not settle for being "so-so" in anything. "Jimmy, don't be mediocre," he'd say. "Whether it's athletics, academics, or personally, don't live life to be average. If athletics at UO win, then the journalism school and law school and the rest of the university win." He always believed that the two realms—athletics and academics—could complement instead of compete against each other.

"Oregon," he'd say, "needs to be more than a line between California and Washington."

I arrived on campus the same year, 1994, that Dave Frohnmayer replaced Myles Brand as president of the university, the two of us about to be blessed with an amazing sense of timing. I'd begun working for UO just when its football stock began to rise, in 1989, and started working in Eugene—associate athletic director of external relationships was my title—just when our stock shot through the roof.

I thank defensive back Kenny Wheaton for that. On October 22, 1994, at Autzen Stadium, Oregon had its back to the wall against Washington. What else was new? For years, the Ducks had played the Huskies tough but somehow UW would find a way to win. In 1984, in fact, Oregon had held Washington to only three first downs—in Seattle no less—and still managed to lose. Now, as the shadows lengthened at Autzen, it looked like the 100th verse, same as the first.

UO quarterback Danny O'Neil had led the Ducks on an improbable 98-yard touchdown drive to give Oregon a 24-20 lead with only 2:40 to play. But Washington moved efficiently downfield, arriving on the Oregon eight yard-line with just over a minute left to play. For Duck fans, it was like watching the same horror movie for the umpteenth time, the one where the hero not only dies in the end, but dies painfully, in humiliation, at the hands of his killer. Pat Kilkenny, a large donor and a future UO athletic director, couldn't watch; he left his sky suite and started to head down to the locker room to support Coach Brooks after a loss that looked to him as inevitable.

Then it happened. Washington quarterback Damon Huard flung the ball toward the near corner of the east end zone. Wheaton stepped in front of the outstretched arms of the receiver, intercepted, and headed for the other end zone. The Ducks won 31-20. It might forever be remembered as the finest fifteen seconds in the history of Oregon athletics.

At the time, I was standing below the goal posts on the west end, my back to thousands of Husky fans, as Washington's offense readied for what nearly everyone thought was going to be a game-winning touchdown. I remember Wheaton running toward me like that *Chariots of Fire* scene when the slow-motion runners are on the beach. He crossed the goal line, came to the back of the end zone, and fell over backward in joyful exhaustion, right at my feet.

Kilkenny missed the entire play.

The victory would not only change the course of the rivalry—Oregon would win 17 of the next 21 games between the two teams—but propel UO to its first Rose Bowl appearance since 1957. In short, Wheaton's interception—immortalized as simply "The Pick"—changed UO football fortunes overnight.

But even that might be understating the consequences of the Ducks' win. You could argue that the unlikely turnaround helped shift Oregon athletics from the mentality of "win-a-few-lose-a-few" to the mentality of "let's-win-championships." And, in so doing, helped ramp up the university's profile in general to a new level.

If Oregon had lost that game, Brooks might have been fired at season's end, the indoor practice facility might not have been built, and a lot of other things that happened might not have. That game was clearly the turning point in Oregon athletics. After Brooks left to accept a job in the NFL, his talented offensive coordinator, Mike Bellotti, took over and kept the momentum pushing forward; a year later he had the Ducks in the Cotton Bowl against Colorado.

The result? People took renewed interest in Oregon's potential. Some people get so wrapped up in "the moment" that they overlook what that moment might mean to the future. Not Phil. He always looks to the future. He is a visionary. Shortly after Wheaton crossed that goal line, he wasn't sticking that moment in his mind's scrapbook. Instead, he was using it as leverage for the future. Dreaming about more.

"Jimmy, this could be just the start," he told me. "There's a lot of sky left to climb."

At the time, it had been fifteen years since Knight's Nike stock went public and he'd awakened with a worth of $178 million. He'd become a billionaire. And while he still loved his business, I sensed he was positioning himself for a new adventure—and it involved his alma mater.

At the time, I was twenty-nine and, for the most part, life was good. Eileen and I had a house built and marveled at the birth of our son, A.J., in 1996. But, for me, "good" always came with an asterisk beside it. I still struggled with insomnia. Still found myself sleeping on a couch at 3 AM. Still saw the face of Stephen Kiesle every time a priest offered me Communion. During a meeting, the slightest mention of something— a name sounding like "Kiesle," for example—could trigger an emotional tailspin within me.

I would start sweating. My heart would start racing. My hands would start shaking. I don't know how many times I excused myself from meetings, ostensibly to use the restroom, so people wouldn't notice such symptoms. Once in the bathroom, I'd look in the mirror but if the guy doing the staring was thirty, the little boy staring back was always eight.

And still scared as hell.

Chapter 6

If Phil's question—*why not shoot higher?*—was about looking to the future in regard to Oregon athletics, my personal question was about looking to the past in regard to my own life: "Why can't I tell anyone?"

In the years since the abuse, I had never mentioned it to my college buddies, not even with a few beers under my belt. I hadn't told the person who I was now sharing my life with, Eileen, the person with whom you'd think I should be an open book. And I certainly wasn't about to share it with my friends, colleagues, or—heaven forbid—a priest at my church.

Though I didn't do lots of soul-searching at the time, I now realize there were lots of reasons for my continued silence. For starters, to search that soul was to be reminded of what had happened. And to be reminded of what had happened, I subconsciously believed, was to only deepen the pain, heighten the guilt, increase the shame.

Deep down, I believed I was damaged goods. It didn't matter if, intellectually, I knew it wasn't my fault. Because deep down, maybe part of me *did* believe it was my fault. How many children grow up believing— and, deep down, still believe as adults—that they caused their parents' divorce? What's more, who was going to tell me otherwise—that I wasn't to blame?

As an adult, I didn't read books about child sex abuse. I didn't watch the few movies that dealt with the subject. I didn't seek professional help. Thus, in the absence of information and empathy that might have broadened, and sharpened, my perspective, I muddled through the best I could. I'd have a couple of glasses of wine at lunch, a couple more to help me sleep. I consumed myself with work. I enjoyed my new role as a father. And I raised the shields of denial around folks at work, the side facing inside toward me marked "shame," the side facing outside to others marked "success."

"Those who attempt to describe the atrocities that they have witnessed … risk their own credibility," writes Judith Herman, author of *Trauma and Recovery.* "To speak publicly about one's knowledge of atrocities is to invite the stigma that attaches to victims … . Denial, repression, and dissociation operate on a social, as well as an individual level."

At twenty-seven, I had become among the youngest NCAA Division I associate athletic directors. Three years later, I had become Oregon's go-to guy when it came to partnering with one of the most influential philanthropists in the country, Phil Knight. And Oregon was starting to catch national attention from people because of our Rose Bowl appearance, new indoor practice facility, and plans to expand the stadium.

Later, when the scales fell off my eyes regarding my abuse, I would come to redefine what success actually is. I would realize that too many people, especially men, think it's only about power, money, position, performance, and prestige—what others think of us. But, back then, I was as susceptible to such shallow thinking as the next guy.

If you blend power, money, position, performance, and prestige, you can create a potent batch of pride soup. But pride does little for lonely men when they're suddenly by themselves. Or, as in my case, when they awaken in the middle of the night, feeling totally alone, because they're holding a secret nobody else knows. Or after everyone else leaves the bar and it's just you and a bartender. At such times, pride is no friend. But, again, I didn't realize that twenty-five years ago. Instead, I played the game, unaware that in life the scoreboard could show you winning even though, deep down, you knew you were far behind.

Why else didn't I talk about what had happened to me—even decades after it occurred? Lots of reasons—again, not that I recognized them at the time. Some of those reasons related to how much time had passed since the abuse occurred nearly twenty-five years ago. That led to a couple of things.

I started questioning my memory. I had nothing, and nobody, to affirm what had happened to me. In relation to this part of my life, I lived in a vacuum. I had no contact with others who had been abused by the man—not even Robbie, the boy who would often be abused by Kiesle in the same interaction I was. No support group to say, "Yeah, we know just how you feel; the memory starts to dim as you age, but that doesn't change the fact that you were exploited. That it *happened*." I had none of that—support, solidarity, someone to share my burden with.

With the passage of time, I wondered if my mind was playing tricks on me. As an adult, you find it more difficult to put yourself in the shoes of an eight-year-old boy being abused by a full-grown man. In other words, the edges of this "abuse of power" get frayed, the focus of once-sharp memories grow fuzzy.

"One reason why men frequently have difficulty thinking of themselves as victims is that in recalling the abuse they mentally picture themselves as men rather than as boys," writes Mic Hunter in *Abused Boys*. "Therefore, I ask my clients to bring in photographs of themselves and, if possible, of the offending person(s) to help them recall more accurately the boy's size and build differences that existed. This helps put the power differential in perspective."

Therapists will often say that the earlier the abuse takes place in a person's life the more severe its impact will be when the person is an adult. Given that my abuse took place from ages seven through ten, it's understandable to me now—writing this book more than forty years later—why it didn't just go away like a bad case of poison oak.

Given all these reasons to keep silent, it's also understandable why I dissociated from what had happened. It's easier to stuff that box in a far corner of the attic so I could forget about it than deal with it. Why own something so repulsive? Over the years, if I heard of a guy who'd been abused as a kid, my response was apt to be: "Must be tough for guys who go through that." But not: "It's tough for *me* to go through this." Such is the power of dissociation. *I'm not one of them.*

But, deep inside, the more I tried to forget about it, the more I realized I couldn't. And the vicious cycle repeated. The cherry on the top of this dessert of denial, of course, was the latent shame I felt for having been abused and for having lied to my parents about it. People with an excess of shame often have unrealistic expectations for themselves, some therapists contend. They believe they need to compensate for something, even if they don't know what that *something* is. Either they have low self-esteem and don't think they do anything well (that wasn't me) or believe they must do everything perfectly (that was *definitely* me).

Realistically, did I have much chance to save the life of Lynn Rosenbach, the WSU associate athletic director? No. Did I nevertheless find a way to feel partly responsible for his death? Yes. "Victim grandiosity" it's called. And I think I probably was suffering from some of that in the 1990s, part of it being my natural inclination to please and part of it being my abuse-triggered shame that exacerbated that tendency.

Frankly, I also think I was plain lonely at times. For anyone who knows me, that will sound strange. I was a husband and father who loved Eileen and A.J. And each day I went to a job that I liked immensely, a job that required me to deal with an array of people, from department members to donors to the media. But loneliness, I found, isn't about how many people you surround yourself with, it's about whether your connectedness to those people can encourage you and make you feel welcome and safe. And though I would feel that support from most of those people, most of the time, there was this inevitable sense of disconnect with them whenever I struggled with my memories of abuse. Because I was the only one who knew. It wasn't their fault they couldn't help me; how can you help someone when that someone doesn't disclose his struggles? So, my silence was like a triple-double of pain: I felt pain for experiencing what I did, I felt shame for not sharing it with anyone, and I felt lonely—often hopeless—because nobody knew but me.

It was always me, alone, against this undefined enemy—not necessarily Kiesle or the Catholic Church, and certainly not my parents who, some might say, allowed me to be in harm's way. (Not in the least.) No, the enemy was never that easily defined or seen or understood. It was just this "it-happened" thorn that seemed forever stuck in my side.

And I had no tools whatsoever to remove it.

In 1995 Bill Moos succeeded Dan Williams, Oregon's interim athletic director. I loved the hire, not the least of which was because, like me, Moos had attended, and later worked for, Washington State University. As associate athletic director at WSU, Moos had hired me to be assistant marketing director, a job I held briefly before moving to Oregon. I respected him highly. Phil liked him, too.

Bill was charismatic, driven, and committed to helping Oregon get to the next level. He was good with the media, good with donors, good with his staff. He had a great sense of humor and, as a former lineman at WSU, a great physical presence: big but in good shape. He seemed a good fit for Phil Knight, as if the two might complement each other well and do great things together. And they would.

But as the new millennium approached and arrived, as we intensified talks about expanding Autzen Stadium, Oregon athletics was entering a new era. If "The Pick" began the revolution in Oregon football it was "The Question" that energized it. It was asked by Knight. And, interestingly, it didn't come in the wake of good times, but in dark times.

On New Year's Day 1996, Oregon was embarrassed in the Cotton Bowl by Colorado, 38-6, the salt in the wound a fourth-quarter fake punt called by Buffaloes coach Rick Neuheisel that worked. *Ouch.* As high as the Ducks had been the previous year, they were low at the end of this one. The weather in Dallas mirrored the mood: cold, windy, rainy. There couldn't have been a more depressing ending to what otherwise was a great season.

At a private party that night at the Dallas hotel where the team was staying, a bunch of folks were chatting over drinks—Moos was there along with Bellotti; Randy Papé, president of the successful heavy-equipment company and a huge friend of Oregon athletics; and Kilkenny, another big donor. Knight sipped his drink and eyed Bellotti.

"So, Mike, what do we need to get to the next level?"

"That's easy, an indoor practice facility," said Bellotti, like me an ex-Californian who knew how Oregon's rain could discourage sunny-state athletes from choosing the UO and how difficult it could be preparing for bowl games in the wet and cold of December. "It'd be a huge boost for recruiting."

"And how long will it take?"

"To fundraise something like that, well, I'd say—."

"No, to *build* it. Get it in place. Have it ready to go. *Use* it."

The eyes around the room widened. Knight wasn't pussyfooting around. Forget the fundraising, he sounded as if he'd like UO to break ground in the morning.

I don't remember the discussion including how much such a facility would even cost. Phil was far more interested in results than processes.

"Whatever it runs," he said, "I'm in for half."

"I'm in for a million," said Kilkenny.

Papé added a thumbs-up, matching that in a few days.

As people were leaving the table, Knight looked at me. "Jimmy," he said, "Let's make this happen."

It was as close to a welcome-to-the-big-leagues moment as I'd experienced. I flew home the next day. That evening, around midnight, Kilkenny called and patched me into a three-way conversation with him and former UO golfer Peter Jacobsen, who was playing in a tournament overseas. Peter was not only in for $1 million but would, in time, put together an annual Legends of Oregon golf tournament that would raise millions for the athletic department. Bottom line, in the week since Phil raised the idea in Dallas, we'd raised pretty much what we needed for the $8 million facility. Soon, a handful of us were on a private jet, checking out other schools' indoor facilities: Kansas State, Notre Dame, Indiana, and Purdue among them.

The decision marked Knight's renewed enthusiasm for Oregon

football. He had always been an Oregon sports fan, but it wasn't until the Rose Bowl appearance that his interest was piqued regarding how much higher the Ducks might fly. And it wasn't until after the Cotton Bowl that he actually made a giant commitment. At this point in his career, he had passed on the baton to others at Nike and was transferring much of his time, energy, and money to the UO. I worked closely with him, keeping him apprised of our progress, of team information, of whatever he wanted or needed. But I always reminded myself: *Don't forget the others.* As much as Knight was a powerful engine on the Duck train, he couldn't do it alone, nor did he want to. He always saw himself as the financial inspiration but never wanted to carry the full load.

Our new indoor practice facility—the Moshofsky Center, named in honor of donors Ed and Elaine Moshofsky—would be built and ready to be used in less than two years. Then we set our sights even higher—on the expansion of Autzen Stadium. Working in UO athletics in these years was like being on a bullet train; you hardly knew where you were at any given time, but wherever you were going, you were getting there fast.

I was arriving early, staying late, shaking hands, smiling, trying to keep everybody happy. For relaxation I socialized. Went to parties. And what did I do there? Talked about work. The line between work and home started getting so blurry I forgot what that line even looked like. Not that Eileen wasn't busy herself. When A.J., our son, had been born on Christmas Day 1996, she was putting in seventy-five-hour weeks as general manager at Shorewood Packaging in Springfield. With A.J.'s arrival, we'd hired a nanny whom we shared with another family.

More challenges arrived. While in Hawaii for the Aloha Bowl in December 1998, I started violently vomiting every night. I don't even remember the game, which is probably good since that was yet another painful loss to Colorado after a furious fourth-quarter rally fell short. On the flight home, I felt terrible—and not because of the game. I was sick. Really sick.

Back home, I was initially diagnosed with irritable bowel syndrome. But that didn't prove to be the case. After three months of doctors scratching their heads and me getting sick nearly every night, they found a mass that was officially deemed to be "eosinophilia," in which the body produces a higher-than-normal level of a type of white blood cell. At worst, it morphs into leukemia. And one of the things that brings it on is stress. My weight plummeted from 160 to 119 pounds.

The good news was that the mass was benign and could be reduced with steroids; no surgery would be required.

"Everything OK at work?" my primary care physician asked.

"Great."

"And at home?"

"Fine."

"You're exhausted, Jimmy. Get some sleep. Eat better. Slow down."

I did. For about a week. Deep inside, the mantra continued: *Never mind how badly you're wounded, soldier. Your war is never over. And the way you protect yourself is to keep your cards close to the vest, at home, in the doctor's office, at work, everywhere. Keep pretending you're the master fixer, the guy who keeps everyone happy. Meanwhile, keep pushing that Father Steve box farther back into the attic, way back, behind all the Duck memorabilia. Maybe then you can forget about it altogether.*

Chapter 7

Phil Knight was a dreamer. His ability to think big was what helped him establish Nike as the world's largest athletic-shoe and apparel company. And it began with him casting off conventional thinking and daring to go where others have never gone. Too many people look at him and see only his ten-digit next worth. They don't know his backstory. His grit. His tenacity. They don't see how he fought to make his dream come true regarding Nike.

If initially awestruck by Phil and Penny, my regard for them morphed into deep respect. A lot of far-less-successful people act as if they're God's gift to humanity. But the Knights never struck me as the type of people who used their money to convince others—or, for that matter, themselves—that they were better than anyone.

As I got to know Phil and his history better, I understood where his humility came from: his beginnings with Nike. He was a fresh-from-business-school (Stanford) graduate who began selling shoes from the back of a Plymouth Valiant. His business made $8,000 its first year; it took him ten years to reach a million dollars in sales. He could have quit and gone to work for some big company. But he'd always relished the idea of taking the unconventional route, of taking the path less traveled, of scrapping and scraping to see if he could make something happen that nobody thought was possible.

In that spirit, he began dreaming of an Oregon football team someday playing for a national championship. In a world of schools such as Florida, Alabama, USC, Ohio State, and Michigan, such talk might have seemed ludicrous at the time. After all, it hadn't been that long ago—1975—that Oregon had a fourteen-game losing streak, at the time the longest stretch of futility in the nation. When UO finally won a game, against Utah, only 10,500 fans sprinkled Autzen Stadium; three out of four seats were empty.

"Maybe today we should introduce the fans to the players before the game," quipped Don McLeod, an *Oregonian* columnist, from the press box. "It'd be faster."

At the time there was talk among California schools that the then-Pac-8 Conference might be better off if Oregon, Oregon State, and Washington State left to play in a lower conference; were they really worthy to stay? A trip to the Rose Bowl in 1995 and appearances in the Cotton Bowl, Sun Bowl, and Holiday Bowl in subsequent years suggested a resurgence for Oregon; still, talk of a national title appearance seemed like pie-in the-often-cloudy Oregon sky.

But if nobody else believed, Phil did. And so did a cluster of others, myself included, though not with the absolute faith he had. I knew Oregon could become a power, but I had a hard time seeing us in a national championship game.

To achieve this national prominence, we realized we couldn't think like everybody else. We couldn't use the same approach at Oregon that the traditional powers were using. It just wouldn't work. We didn't have the history that schools such as Ohio State and Alabama used to sell recruits. Didn't have hundreds of blue-chip players within a twenty-five-mile radius of campus like USC and UCLA. And didn't have the first-rate facilities—stadiums, weight rooms, and locker rooms—that tended to impress recruits.

But there was another foundational reason our athletic programs were underdogs back then: the lack of state financial support for the university. In 1990, Oregonians narrowly passed Ballot Measure 5, which severely cut the property-tax revenues that Oregon schools relied on as their principle form of funding. In essence, it left the state's colleges to fend for themselves, the first state to all but abandon higher education. When the state cut its funding for higher education by 10.5 percent, President Frohnmayer told our faculty in October 1994 that the university would have to dig that much deeper with donors to remain viable as a university. Overnight, big donors—people such as Knight—became all the more important to the viability of our university.

Such a backdrop only accentuated the sense that the University of Oregon was crazy for thinking it could one day play for a national championship in football. But, then, I remember what Phil had said he'd been thinking the first time he flew to Japan, in 1962, to see if he could swing a deal for the Japanese to make shoes for him: *Maybe I was ... crazy.*

And maybe we needed to be a little crazy, too. So, we decided to take a risk. We would upgrade and add facilities, the likes of which nobody else had seen. In 1999, to seed that dream, the Knights promised $30 million for the expansion of the south side of Autzen Stadium, which would increase the seating from 41,000 to about 53,000 and help us increase our yearly revenues substantially. What's more, we began talking about adding a state-of-the-art locker room, complete with computer jacks for each player and flat-screen televisions. But what ultimately made the biggest difference, beyond winning more games in the next three years than any such span in school history, was this: turning the country on its ear with our wild new uniforms and helmets.

Oregon's shtick, we decided, would be innovation and creativity. The new approach not only fit with UO's liberal arts foundation and sports marketing school, but our propensity for being slightly wacky, our school mascot being a duck and our cinematic claim to fame being the filming site for the raucous 1978 comedy *Animal House.*

In Beaverton, a trio of Nike folks went to work on designing the new-look Ducks. By the time ex-UO pole vaulter Tinker Hatfield, Todd Van Horne, and Mike Doherty—and their staffs—were finished, Oregon's players looked more like superheroes than football players. The interlocking "UO" was gone, replaced—thanks to Nike designer Rick Bakas—by a single, simple "O" whose exterior was shaped like Autzen Stadium and interior like storied Hayward Field. The color green got darker, like a mallard duck, and the yellows brighter, like the bold, wide ink of a Highlighter pen. The jerseys had stripes down their sides. The helmets, green, featured a metallic finish that nobody else in the country was using. Even the material used for the uniforms was cutting-edge, a new type of Lycra made with a fabric called Cordura.

All of this wasn't going to be an easy sell to the seventy-five-year-old Duck loyalists who'd been backing us since the rainy 1970s when they'd show up in Glad trash bags with holes popped in the tops and sides. But when we envisioned an eighteen-year-old football recruit reacting to them, we liked our chances. And we were right. We did take some heat from World War II generation fans. One donor came up to me after a Duck Club meeting.

"Jimmy, what the hell you guys smoking over there at the Cas Center? Are you serious?" *Register-Guard* letters to the editor rolled in from folks who thought that messing with the interlocking "UO" was nothing short of sacrilegious.

But I was right about the recruits. They liked the new look. And to make sure they saw the new uniforms, we worked out a deal with the YES television network in New York City—and, two years later, with ESPN Regional—to air our games; granted, they were on in the middle of the night but, for the first time, recruits had the chance to see every one of our games.

If a lot of older fans grumbled about the new look, I figured we could win over the traditionalists on the scoreboard; nobody would grumble about uniforms if they were attracting recruits who were helping us beat Washington, Oregon State, and an occasional non-conference stalwart. In a splash of good fortune, Oregon's 1999 team had a solid first season in the new garb—9-3 with a come-from-behind win in the Sun Bowl led

Top: Our home in Pinole, California, where I grew up. Though this is a 2019 photo—our garage didn't have windows back in the 1970s—I still look at it and see Dodger Stadium, where I played lots of make-believe baseball games. Above: I'm eight in the baseball photos— about six months after the abuse began.

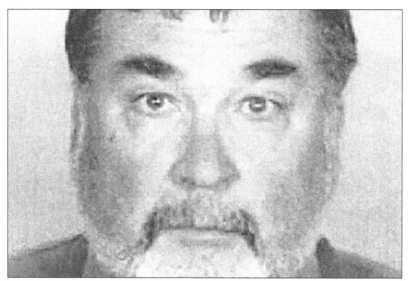

Top: Father Steve Kiesle after his arrest in 1978 in connection with the molestations of six children. Right: Robbie and I, two of the more than a hundred children Kiesle would abuse. Left: Pope Benedict XVI, earlier known as Cardinal Joseph Ratzinger, stalled on granting Kiesle's request to be defrocked, writing that it could provoke "detriment ... within the community of Christ's faithful."

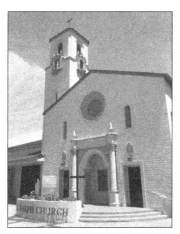

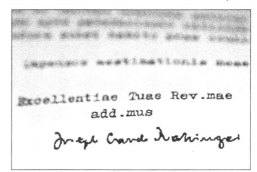

Top: The St. Joseph rectory where the abuse usually took place. Above, left: The church. Above, right: Signature on the letter, written in Latin, by then-Cardinal Joseph Ratzinger to the Diocese of Oakland saying Kiesle should not be defrocked without further study. Ratzinger later became the pope.

Top: As a Washington State football manager, my "stride-in-stride" moment with Michigan's Bo Schembechler in the "Big House" in 1983. Above, left, my folks, Jim and Mary Jane, in the 1990s. Above, me and A.J.

I couldn't have been prouder of Danielle, when, as fifth-grader, she stepped up to be the "family" of University of Oregon basketball player Carlos Emory on Senior Day.

Top: On the field with Chip Kelly, the hurry-up Oregon football coach who helped Duck football rise to all-new levels. Above: A.J. and Danielle in the new Matthew Knight Arena in January 2011.

Dave Frey

Dave Frey

Top: Phil Knight and another huge Duck booster, Ken O'Neil, celebrate another UO score in a 31-27 upset of Michigan at Autzen Stadium in 2003. Above: No matter how exciting the event, the memory of Father Steve Kiesle was never too far away for me.

Top: In 2012, Danielle and I celebrate Oregon's 45-38 win over Wisconsin in the Rose Bowl. Above: Phil Knight waves to the crowd at Matthew Knight Arena, named for his son.

by quarterback Joey "Captain Comeback" Harrington. Had we rolled out the new look and gone 2-10, who knows what would have happened to Oregon football.

Initially, we took lots of flak from people around the country; Oregon, they said, had *the worst uniforms ever!* The Ducks were a joke. (And, I admit, I wasn't thrilled with every new look.) But when other schools started copying us, the tide shifted. Imitation, of course, is the sincerest form of flattery. When enough schools changed their uniforms and started looking like us, we'd come up with a different look, a look that would be unique—until the copying resumed. Then we'd repeat the approach again and again and again. In seasons to come, we became like a high-jumper who kept setting the bar higher and higher—and clearing each height. We kept adding innovation to our innovation, always changing things up, zigging when people thought we might zag.

The result? For the first time, the University of Oregon was becoming something special, distinguished, unique in the eyes of the nation. In short, it was becoming its own brand. That might sound cold and commercial, as if the school were nothing but a product to be advertised and sold. Not the case. A brand, when kept in perspective, can be a means to a greater end, a way to draw interest to your school so you can improve your academic offerings, so more students will want to attend the school, and so more donors will want to support it. Isn't that the idea? To provide the best academic and athletic education possible? To find people who, in a time when the state had essentially turned its back on higher education, could help the university not only stay afloat but afford better professors and better facilities? To improve what it offers young people?

Early mornings. Late nights. Out-of-the-box thinking. It was a wild time, though I loved it for reasons beyond Oregon becoming more relevant on a national level. I loved it because it was a wonderful distraction. But then something would happen to snap the "spell." Among such tripwires: seeing the altar boys at church. I'd been one of them back in Pinole, where the demons wanted to drag me back to. The rectory. The bedroom. The wine. The—

"Dad, dad," A.J. would whisper. "Can we watch Kobe Bryant and the Lakers this afternoon?"

"You bet. Let's go."

In 1998, beyond being in charge of the Duck Athletic Fund, the equipment room, and men's and women's golf teams, I officially became associate athletic director for community and corporate relations. That's what the whole university-donor dance is all about. There's a relationship between athletics and academics. The two can help each other. Complement each other. Encourage each other. Or, with leadership that overlooks this obvious opportunity, each pursuit can try to make it on their own, work against each other, weaken one another.

Having been involved in fundraising much of my career, I can tell you, point blank, that raising money the week after a big football win—for strictly academic purposes—is far easier than raising money the week after a loss. The cynic might see that as donors being shallow and the institute being exploitative. The realist sees that as a wonderful opportunity to improve both academics and athletics. As they say: "All boats rise on an incoming tide."

Phil was adamant about this. And his track record showed it. Yes, he and Penny had donated graciously to Oregon athletics. But they had also donated graciously to academics through the remodeling of the library, the building of a new law school, and the endowment of professorships. The Knights were anything but a one-trick pony featuring Oregon athletics as their lone focus. Beyond UO, they've given hundreds of millions to cancer research. They've given hundreds of millions to the school where Phil got his advanced degree in business, Stanford. And they've given millions to help people in ways nobody even hears about.

"We should be excellent in the classroom and we should be excellent in the athletic venues," Phil loved to say.

Which brings us back to our new football uniforms. They were creativity-in-motion. They drew attention. And when our teams won while wearing them, they strengthened our connection to students looking for a school and donors looking to invest their money to some greater cause.

That's why Oregon began taking chances by being "out there." And that's why, before the 2003 game against Oregon State, I was in our Autzen Stadium football locker room with scissors and double-sided tape. The team had warmed up in a green-and-yellow combination but came out for the game in a black-on-black accented by a diamond-plating look. It wasn't easy. Football uniforms take a lot of time to get off and on; our equipment people didn't initially like the idea, suggesting we wouldn't have time to make the switch. But the more the Nike marketing team explained the idea, the more the ice thawed.

"OK," said equipment manager Pat Conrad, "tell me what you need, and we'll get it done."

We assembled a group of a dozen "quick-change" helpers, including my six-year-old son A.J. and my brother-in-law, Keith, and his son, Drew, who were ready with scissors and double-stick tape—scissors to cut off the old uniforms that we were going to retire anyway and tape to keep the players' shoulder pads stuck to their jerseys. We were like the pit crew at the Indianapolis 500, making the transition in less than five minutes. As the team headed for the tunnel, we celebrated with high-fives.

It was a foggy Saturday night and when the Ducks burst onto the field, Autzen went wilder than usual, which is pretty wild; already, some were mentioning the stadium as one of the toughest places in the country to play. The Ducks' Jonathan Stewart took the opening kickoff 99 yards to the house and we went on to win 56-14, one of the most lopsided outcomes in the history of what we called the "Civil War."

The guy who never got as much credit as he deserved for such innovation was Bellotti, who could have told the innovators to back off, that what wins football games was running, passing, blocking, and tackling. But he didn't. Even when it meant a frenetic wardrobe change right before the Civil War, he trusted that the new uniforms were a means to a greater end, even if he did joke that his players were spending way too much time in front of the mirror.

As much as I enjoyed Oregon's new creative bent—and added some ideas of my own— my main role in this venture was helping us run with the ideas and being the liaison to Phil Knight. By now my phone number was the one he punched when he wanted to talk about anything involving the UO. If he and I had developed a close business relationship, he and Penny and I had developed an even closer friendship. We dined together. Traveled to games together. Went to Duck gatherings together.

In any endeavor, there are those who dream the dream and those who come alongside that person and help them achieve those dreams. I was more than content to be the latter—the wingman, the guy in the shadows, the support van. It's a skill I'd learned at Washington State as the football team's manager, and a skill, frankly, that not enough people appreciate. Too many want to be the lead dog on the sled when their skill set, disposition, and passion are to serve others from beyond the limelight.

The only problem with support-van folks is this: who's there for them if they blow a tire? Who picks them up when they fall? Who cares for the caregivers, especially the ones who are hurting but are afraid to tell anyone? Down the road I'd have a chance to find my answer. But first I was about to be called in to help heal a relational split that threatened the very future of the University of Oregon.

Nobody saw this one coming, least of all me.

Chapter 8

Dave Frohnmayer, the university president, was an exceptional leader, the rare person at that level who was wonderful with donors, good with the media, and respected by most of the faculty and students. He even enthusiastically taught a class on leadership. And was secure enough in himself to realize that every idea didn't need to be his idea, every approach didn't need to be his approach.

As such, he welcomed our new bent toward creativity. Frohnmayer and Phil were, in some ways, polar opposites. Phil arrived at UO games from Portland in a personal jet; Dave drove a minivan. Phil hobnobbed with the likes of Michael Jordan and Tiger Woods; Dave raked his own leaves at his house near the university. But the two shared great respect for the UO and for one man—Bill Bowerman, Nike's co-founder.

Frohnmayer's father, Otto, a Medford attorney who died in 2000, had been a close friend of Bowerman's; Bill had grown up in Medford. The two families used to vacation together at Central Oregon's Cultus Lake.

Swanky uniforms and upscale locker rooms might have seemed "out there" to Frohnmayer, but he knew a good thing when he saw it. And he trusted the Knights' devotion to UO was genuine. In 1994 they had given $27.4 million to renovate and expand a library that was renamed in the family's honor. They had begun endowing some professorships.

Frohnmayer's passion, at its core, was the education of students. But with the state taking on less and less of the financial burden, the UO's situation was turning dark. If football could help draw more students and inspire more donors, that would put more money in the university coffers. But just as the need for the support of people like Knight was at an all-time high, he and the university had a fallout.

Since 1997, some universities had been protesting Nike's—and other such apparel companies'—overseas factories and their alleged exploitation of workers. Now, in the spring of 2000, a group of students called on President Frohnmayer to support the Worker Rights Consortium (WRC), a student-led organization that had already signed on dozens of universities to hold businesses such as Nike more accountable with overseas workers. To punctuate their protest, students held a sit-in April 4 at Johnson Hall, the UO's administrative center. Among other things, the WRC demanded that the school not support the more industry-friendly Fair Labor Association (FLA) organization, which had been formed by the Clinton administration under the leadership of Secretary of Labor Robert Reich. The FLA was a partnership of government and companies that sourced overseas.

Nike felt that the WRC, having been formed as a partnership of Big Labor and student activities, was biased against foreign trade in general and Nike in particular; the group referred to Knight as the most evil of company CEOs. Knight's company sent out a memo to its major college endorsers requesting they not join the WRC, but rather the FLA.

Frohnmayer was between a rock and a hard place. Knight and many other business leaders with ties to the UO obviously preferred the FLA. The students, even if representing only a portion of UO students, were protesting long and hard for the WRC. That alone stressed Frohnmayer, but, at fifty-nine he was also dealing with prostate cancer—after having had a heart attack the previous year. In April 2000, he flew to the Mayo Clinic in Minnesota regarding his cancer. When he returned, the protests ramped up a notch. The students and faculty weren't going away on this one.

A week later, I picked up Phil and his "Duck entourage" of six people at the Eugene Airport so he could watch a UO football practice. He loved the intricacies of the football program. When our annual media guide came off the press, we'd overnight the first copy to him and he'd study it with diligence. He knew players' names. He knew the team's history. He knew our schedule. He'd call me two or three times a week just to talk football.

"What recruits are visiting this weekend?" he'd say. He loved talking to coaches, followed recruiting, even memorized the names and numbers of guys on the team so he could personally greet them.

After the practice, he threw back a few beers with the coaches and me, laughed heartily at the banter, said his goodbyes, and flew back to Portland. The next morning, he called. I could feel the tension in his voice from ninety miles away

"Jimmy, did we really just sign on to back the WRC?"

What? I didn't know what he was talking about; I hadn't even looked at the morning's *Register-Guard*. Wait, could this be some sort of prank? He'd been known to pull one on occasion.

It wasn't a prank, I soon learned.

When I confirmed with his assistant that it was true, Phil's communication with us shut down. Somehow, Oregon was on the verge of losing the largest donor in the history of the school—at a time when we needed him most. And it happened in the time it took Dave Frohnmayer to sign his name to the WRC agreement to become a dues-paying member.

THE LAST TIME my heart had raced like this after a phone call I'd been thirteen years old and my mother was asking me if my basketball coach had hurt me in any way. Now thirty-five, sitting in my desk at the Cas Center, I buried my face in my hands, my first instinct to run and hide.

After all, that's what I'd been doing much of my life, the only thing keeping me afloat being a job that serendipitously played to the thing I did best: keep the customers satisfied.

"Bill, we gotta meet pronto, with the staff," I said with a quick call to Moos. "Phil says Oregon is linking with the WRC."

"I just heard."

Howard Slusher, Phil's right-hand man, had left Moos a phone message in which he reamed the athletic director mercilessly for letting this happen. A few moments later, after Moos barked an order, chairs slid. Doors opened. Half a dozen people huddled in a conference room, all now aware of what had happened, all with ashen looks on their faces. The media didn't have the story yet, but it was true: Frohnmayer had agreed to allow the UO to join the WRC and Phil, it appeared, was cutting ties with the university.

I called Phil's long-time assistant, a woman who knew me by voice, to talk to him. There was a chill in her voice. "He's, uh, not ready to talk to anyone right now."

"Well, tell him I called. Tell him I'd love to talk to him. Maybe we can work something out."

I stuck my head in Moos's office. "Won't talk to me."

"Keep at it," he said. "See what you can do."

Frohnmayer, I think, had found himself in a no-win situation. Students camped on the front lawn of Johnson Hall for ten days to show their support for the WRC; the faculty senate voted twenty to one to join. Either the president underestimated the repercussions joining would have with Knight and other business owners in terms of donations or he expected serious fallout but believed joining was still the right thing to do. At any rate, he made his decision—a one-year commitment to the WRC—and Knight made his.

"The University of Oregon, despite its unique relationship with Nike and Phil, is free to align itself with the Worker Rights Consortium," Nike's statement read. "However, it does not mean that we are required to support those efforts with which we have fundamental differences."

Knight said the UO had "inserted itself into the new global economy where I make my living. And inserted itself on the wrong side, fumbling a teachable moment. Ask University of Oregon President Dave Frohn-mayer one question. Ask him if he will sign a pledge that all contractors and sub-contractors of the University of Oregon … meet the WRC's 'living wage' provision."

No doubt about it, Phil was playing hard ball.

I left dozens of messages with Phil's assistant in the days to come. No response. None.

FINALLY, DAYS LATER I was home watching ESPN's SportsCenter when the name "Penelope Knight" appeared on my screen, courtesy of Comcast. It was Phil. The gist of his call was this: *Yeah, I'm cutting ties with Oregon and I'm withholding the $30 million for the stadium add-on but I had no other choice. This isn't the way I wanted it to end, Jimmy. Do something, buddy. Do something.*

I sat in my den and mindlessly watched television. I was already having trouble sleeping; this would only make things worse. I sipped a glass of chardonnay. Vented to Eileen more than she deserved. Didn't pay enough attention to A.J., now four.

I kept thinking of Moos's last words: *Keep at it. See what you can do.* I could read between the lines. It was my job to keep Phil in the fold. Bill was a helluva good athletic director, but he and Phil's relationship didn't go deep. Moos knew, and I knew, that there was nothing he could do to broker a peace treaty, short of getting Frohnmayer to reverse his decision. And that wasn't likely. He also knew that, over the years, I'd become Phil's go-to guy and, I think, appreciated me in that role.

I made a few phone calls to folks in "the know," less to impart—or get—information than to remind myself I wasn't alone in all this sudden split, though I clearly felt I was. I leaned back in the La-Z-Boy and stared at the ceiling. For some reason I remembered the day when I was twenty-two and WSU Coach Dennis Erickson and I were trying to pump life into our bleeding associate athletic director, Lynn Rosenbach. From what I'd heard as of late—Phil's call, Slusher's call, Phil's assistant's refusal to forward my call—the patient, like Rosenbach, was already flat-lining. And I had no chance of saving him.

Knight's $30 million was nearly half of the planned $80 million Autzen addition. Without it, we might not be dead in the water, but we'd be flailing. That said, what hurt me so badly wasn't that we might be delayed in expanding a football stadium—or forced to postpone it indefinitely. What hurt me was thinking that the university's special relationship with Phil Knight might be over for good—and my relationship with Phil and Penny might be collateral damage.

In my nearly fifteen years working for the UO, I'd realized that when it comes to philanthropy, the giver-receiver relationship is a sort of magical win-win for the two parties involved. The receivers, of course, get money to improve their school or organization or whatever. But the givers get something, too. Beyond the feel-good knowledge of helping others, the givers get the privilege of being part of something bigger than themselves. They get to "join the family," so to speak, which, in the case of wealthy individuals, translates their money into a sense of belonging.

Yes, whether the "giving arena" is football, academics, ballet, music, or theater, bigger donors get special privileges. And, to be sure, Phil Knight got his share. But, knowing him pretty well by then, I was reasonably sure what would hurt him following this breakup had nothing to do with privilege, access, status, or the like. Instead, it was that he'd miss being part of the Duck family, plain and simple. He'd miss seeing people going nuts at a game because we were winning. In particular, he'd miss the students celebrating a win—and perhaps thinking: *Maybe I had a little something to do with that.*

Even if the UO hadn't spelled it out in hand-written edicts, it was clear that the school was turning to me for some sort of magical fix. I felt a weight on my shoulders that I could hardly bear. For better or worse, I'd spent much of my life trying to keep everyone around me happy, which included *not* telling my folks that their favorite priest had repeatedly molested me for nearly three years.

I'd lied about being abused, risked being bullied by Milton's tormentors, and put my life on the line on icy I-84 driving WSU equipment to games—all to keep people happy. And been glad to do so, even knowing that beneath the surface I was as fragile as a teacup. But now I felt done. Finished. Empty. I bowed my head. Forget all the "official" prayers.

"Help me, God," I prayed. "Please help me. I've got no idea what to do."

Not just about the Frohnmayer-Knight debacle, but about the Jimmy debacle: the boy in the mirror. Regarding the most defining event of my entire life, I had nobody who knew and could offer me encouragement, solace, context. At one time I considered myself "MIA" but I came to realize that didn't fit because you can't be missing in action unless someone knows you're gone. I was gone, I was missing, I was lost in the rubble of war, but nobody knew it but me. And, thus, nobody was about to try to rescue me.

I blamed myself. It was nobody's fault but mine. Because I let it happen to me back then and I didn't dare tell anyone. To tell was to hurt those I loved. My job had always been to make people happy. And the fallout from telling my story now would be far more severe than when the abuse happened. I had my own family to protect. I had friends. I had donors I'd courted for years. I had a university I represented. I had work colleagues all over the country. To admit what happened to me was to risk hurting relationships I'd valued for decades. And yet it was precisely this kind of anxiety that always had, and always would—as long as I kept my secret—take me back to the abuse, where I'd relive the trauma.

I hated to see people hurt, especially people I knew and cared about. Phil and Dave were two of those people. So was the guy looking back at me each night when I glanced in the mirror while brushing my teeth. Now, nearly thirty years after the abuse, I wasn't sure who was more to blame: Kiesle or me. Sure, he'd abused me. But I'd lied. And how many kids had he harmed because of that?

As an adult I'd grappled with why I continued to keep the secret. But why hadn't I told someone when it first happened to me? Why not just go tell my parents that Father Steve was abusing me?

At the time, I didn't even know what abuse was. And even if I did, therapists will tell you that a child has such a limited vocabulary that it's unlikely he or she could tell others even if inclined to do so. Amid the fog of childhood—shrouded in the complexities of Mass and monsters—I was still trying to figure out right from wrong, good from evil, who to trust and who not to trust. And, largely, that cue was coming from the adults in my life: my parents, my teachers, my friends' folks, all of whom—remember—believed Father Steve had arrived in Pinole as if a gift from God.

Robbie, my friend who was abused by Kiesle along with me and with whom I've since reconnected, says the same thing. "We didn't know right from wrong. Yeah, I thought it was weird. But it's complicated. And the fear and shame suggest 'keep quiet.'"

"Bewildered and embarrassed, [victims] retreat into a cocoon of secrecy, the unraveling of which can be painful and protracted," writes Jason Berry, an investigative reporter, in *Lead Us Not into Temptation.*

The abuse can become such a normal part of your life that the line between good and evil gets blurred beyond recognition. I'd read of a woman who was abused for six years by a priest—and yet asked the man to officiate at her wedding. It wasn't that uncommon.

"I buried it all," she said. "I pretended he never came near me." Denial becomes our friend—or so we subconsciously convince ourselves.

Time would prove that Robbie and I were far from Father Steve's only victims. And the reason he got away with his crime was because, for literally decades, nobody told. So, it isn't like I was alone in harboring the secret. Though we might wish otherwise, *this is the default response for children of sex abuse.*

A classmate of my sister's refused—for decades—to tell anyone about being repeatedly abused by Father Steve. When she finally did, thirty years later, her own mother squinted her eyes at her.

"You're a *liar,*" the woman said to her own daughter. "Father Steve was a priest. He couldn't have done that."

It was the mid-1970s when I was abused. Schools didn't talk about the subject. Newspapers didn't write about it. TV didn't air specials on it.

Why didn't you simply run? Or fight back? Or refuse to spend time with him? Again, easy to ask with adult hindsight. But kneel on the floor in front of another adult to simulate the size difference between the two. Now, imagine not only the difference in size and strength, but in the perception of who has power and who does not: parents, coaches, pastors, priests, teachers, law-enforcement officers, judges—to a child, these are the people who set the rules, enforce the rules, and set the punishment for breaking the rules. With such physical and emotional disadvantages, what child dares to question, especially if the abuser plays on the child's fears, embarrassment, guilt—or all three?

"Who would believe you?" an abuser might say. Or as with the monster threat: "If you tell, bad things will happen to you."

Don't get me wrong, I'm not saying my silence was *right*. I'm saying I had little choice. He had the power; I had none. I'm saying that it's far easier to subtly blame the victim for the wrong response than to appreciate the larger context—and to focus on the one who deserves the blame: the abuser. Too often people who haven't been through abuse act as if they know better than a victim how the situation could have easily been avoided. They don't.

Expecting a child to tell on a perpetrator overlooks the many nuances that muddy the waters. Debbie Alexander, a therapist and author of *Children Changed by Trauma*, often sits across from people like me who refused to tell. In fact, decades later, some still haven't forgiven themselves for not telling.

"I give them a homework assignment," she said. "If the abuse happened when they were six or seven, I tell them to sit on a park bench and watch six- or -seven-year-olds play on the playground. Observe them for an hour. Listen to how they talk. They're children. It's unrealistic for others to say, 'Why didn't you just tell someone?'"

In my childhood eyes, Father Steve was a revered man, the closest adult figure to me other than my mother and father. Everyone loved him. Everyone believed in him. Everyone supported him. *Everyone.* Against that kind of bedrock support for the man, no wonder a second-grader might not immediately call foul.

Did I think that what Father Steve was doing to us was wrong? I wasn't sure. Did I think what he was doing to us was strange? Definitely. And did I go about my merry way afterward, as if nothing had happened? Absolutely not. What he did has haunted me every single day of my life.

I became Houdini, an expert in getting out of whatever jam I found myself in. I could be in a meeting with college presidents, superstar athletes, and some of the most influential entrepreneurs in the world when something would trigger a Kiesle memory. My gut would turn to acid. My hands would start to tremble. My legs would begin to shake. But I would always find a way out: a quick trip to the restroom, an "urgent" cell phone call that I needed to make outside the meeting, something to momentarily take me away so I could collect myself and nobody would see the real me. I was so adept at hiding my past that for decades nobody "caught on." I saved my meltdowns for times when I was "off." And I can honestly say I never let the flashbacks affect how I did my job.

I was the master of escape, so good at it that those around me never even knew I was trapped.

Chapter 9

It was now June 2000. The president was taking increasing heat from friends of the university who felt his pro-WRC stance screamed anti-business. But neither side appeared to be budging, even if the UO's general counsel, Melinda Grier, was growing skeptical about the university's legal ground regarding the WRC and digging more deeply for information.

Meanwhile, how nice it would have been to have a playbook that offered all sorts of possibilities for fourth-and-forever situations like this. All I knew was that whatever I did, it would fit under the "Hail Mary" category, a desperation final pass whose chances of success were slim.

In late June, as I was still mulling how to make some sort of inroad with Phil, he called me at home late one night. It was a very strange conversation, as if he desperately wanted to reconnect with Oregon but simply didn't know how. Nike couldn't be seen as playing favorites.

He told me he was hurt, confused, and angry. He loved the University of Oregon but felt a deep loyalty to his company. "It's the principle," he said. "I can't treat Oregon differently than the other schools who have deals with us. You gotta figure something out, OK? Find a way."

It was nice to talk to Phil again—first time in almost two months—but he was again asking for me to pull some sort of rabbit out of a hat. Just like Moos was. I was one guy, an associate athletic director who was part of something way larger. This was a story that had played all over the world. *Figure it out?* What did that even mean?

RELATIONSHIPS. WHILE MULLING the fallout, that's the word that kept coming back to me. I'd come to appreciate it first in Medford at age twenty-two. Donor money just came along for the ride. What the people who gave it—and the institutions that received it—were really about was relationships. *The way in which two or more concepts, objects, or people are connected, or the state of being connected.*

What did Phil need? Not berating. Not ego feeding. Not political leverage. If we were treading water until a solution to this breakup could be found, he needed to know that nobody was holding a grudge against him. That his value to us went beyond his money and political disagreements regarding his business. That we respected him. And, above all, that we *cared* about him—and, of course, Penny. We needed to show that we cared about the two of them even, if for now, we knew they were mad as hell at us. Call it unending respect, unconditional love, whatever you want. But this seemed to be the very stuff of *connection.*

Fine, but a Hallmark card seemed a wimpy way to communicate that. We needed to *show* him. But how? What, more than anything, was the connection to Phil? He loved the school. And, as a former runner for Bowerman, he loved athletics, competition, student-athletes striving for excellence on a track or basketball court or football field.

Football. Oh, how Phil Knight loved football. My mind started whirring as if for the first time in six weeks, when he'd first called and said *do something.* I did something. I called quarterback Joey Harrington and defensive end Saul Patu, who happily agreed to drive to Portland with me and talk football with him. When, finally, I got a message to him, he welcomed us. It was a good time. But not enough.

Back in Eugene, notebook in hand, I brainstormed ideas for what we could do to involve Phil in Oregon football. *Think outside the box, man.* Finally, it came. I went to Moos the next day.

"I've got an idea," I said.

"About what?"

"What we can do to reach out to him."

"I'm listening."

"Televise Duck games this fall."

"Well, sure, there's a handful of games of ours that'll be televised this fall: Wisconsin, a few others."

"No, we televise them *all*—just to Phil and Penny's living room. Nobody else. They'd love it. They'd realize we still consider them part of the family. We're there for them."

Moos winced as if he'd eaten something sour.

"What—Jimmy, are you nuts?"

"No, I'm serious. Think outside the box."

He shook his head with skepticism.

"I've already talked to Scott Chambers at KEZI," I said. "He says they can make it happen."

"Seriously?"

"They're already filming all the games for the coach's shows. And he says they can pipe it just to Phil and Penny—live. We need to figure out a way to keep him connected. Keep him feeling a part of this until—I don't know—he and Dave meet and maybe work this thing out. Or someone figures something out."

Moos pursed his lips. "Hey, if you can do it, do it."

A few days later, Chambers had signed on, though the setup wasn't as simple as I'd originally thought. Chambers sent a technician to Portland to erect a satellite dish at the Knights' house but had to return a second time because Phil and Penny weren't getting the feed.

But come September, the Knights would be the only people on planet Earth to see television coverage of all Duck football games, complete with DuckVision—the stuff shown on the giant screen at the stadium—during commercials.

But that wasn't enough. I had another idea: arrange for Phil to be able to hear Jeff Tedford, our offensive coordinator, make his play calls. Sure, tap him into the headsets for all our games.

"This is a joke, right?" said Moos.

"No, this is doable."

Again, Bill gave me a blessing. "Go for it," he said.

The Ducks' radio broadcaster, Jerry Allen, helped me out because I had no clue how to set this all up. Two-way communication. All games. The Autzen hookup was relatively easy; Jerry could make a one-time connection that could be used for all five home games. But for road games at Wisconsin, USC, and Arizona State, running the wire from our coaches' booth to the radio booth, just before kickoff, always triggered lots of "what-the-hell?" headshakes from reporters and others. But we got it done—and bizarre as it may sound, nobody in the press box ever asked what we were doing.

I later heard that Penny decorated the Knight living room as if it was their skybox. I loved how those two had a lighter side to them; they loved how football was fun. Of course, in the days of being charged by the minute for long-distance calls, some in the UO billing department were growing suspicious of our huge phone bills on Saturdays that fall. But I assured them it was money well spent—with the potential to benefit the university big-time. And our compliance officer had signed-off on everything; there was nothing we did that violated NCAA rules.

"Watch this play," Tedford would say. "You're gonna love it, Phil. I guarantee a first down."

MEANWHILE, I'D COME home at night and Eileen would ask how my day went. "Fine," I'd say.

"Meaning?"

"Usual stuff."

I was a closed book—and had been since 1972. Smile. Schmooze. Be the life of the party if you have to. But never let anybody inside your life, not even your wife. At work, I nurtured relationships with an eye to the uniqueness of the individual and with the goal of making people happy. At home I too often put my relationship with Eileen on automatic pilot. I was deeply involved with A.J.; fatherhood was something I loved and cherished. I coached his teams. Introduced him to Duck stars. Took him on a few trips. But husband-wife relationships only flourish when fortified by a sharing of the "deep stuff" and, at least with the abuse, I couldn't go there.

Father Steve wouldn't let me.

As WE TREADED water with Phil, the university's legal counsel, Grier, was doing homework about the WRC. Soon she had found enough questionable parts of the UO-WRC relationships to advise Frohnmayer to stop paying dues lest the university open itself to liability. For example, Grier, who, in my eyes would become the unsung hero in all this, claimed the WRC had not yet incorporated, had not filed as a non-profit, and served no public purpose justifying a dues payment. In a letter to Frohnmayer, Grier said because the WRC had not been certified as tax-exempt by the IRS and had not filed to form a corporation, the university could be held liable for any lawsuits arising from the group's actions.

Learning such information, Frohnmayer decided it was no longer in the best interest of the UO to remain in the WRC. On October 25, 2000, he announced that the university was no longer paying dues to the WRC.

That thawed the ice with Phil immediately. He hopped on his private jet and flew to Pullman for the Nov. 4 game against Washington State. I arrived on another plane about the same time and it was among the more harrowing landings I've ever been part of—it was snowing hard. But when we got to Martin Stadium most Duck fans began cheering wildly for Phil. He was like a little kid again. He loved being back with the family. Oregon won in overtime, 27-24, to improve to 8-1 on the season.

Would Phil have hung around and returned to the fold had we not reached out to him during that nearly seven months and made him understand we still cared deeply about him? Who knows?

What I do know is that when the controversy settled down, Phil Knight didn't sign a check to the UO for $30 million as he'd planned. He signed a check for $50 million.

We broke ground soon. The new stadium was ready to go in 2002.

Chapter 10

Like the villain in an R-rated horror movie, Stephen Kiesle didn't go away. He apparently hadn't moved away to get a fresh start somewhere else. He remained in the East Bay. He hadn't repented for his sins. Nor had he paid any significant price for those sins. Between the church and the courts, the response to Kiesle's abuse in the 1970s was not about punishing him and keeping children safe. It was, in essence, about offering him an open invitation to strike again.

And he happily obliged.

By the summer of 1995, twenty-three years after he had molested me, Kiesle was forty-eight years old. He had been out of the priesthood for more than a decade, had married Robbie's mother, gone to school at University of California-Berkeley, then gone to work for Chevron. But if much had changed in his life, one thing hadn't. He was still molesting children.

In 2002, a woman alleged to police that Kiesle had sexually abused her while she was a minor in 1995. It happened, she said, at Kiesle's mountain vacation cabin in Tahoe Donner, California. The latter case triggered a month-long investigation by the Fremont Police Department. The girl was my friend Robbie's cousin, the one whose mother Robbie had warned regarding Kiesle—too late, as it turned out.

Eventually, Kiesle faced thirteen criminal charges of molesting young girls. However, eleven of the charges were wiped out when the U.S. Supreme Court, in 2003, struck down a California law that allowed for the prosecution of child molestation suspects within one year after the abuse was *reported*, regardless of how long it'd been since the alleged crime was *committed*. Since 1994, the California law had been used retroactively to prosecute scores of priests and other alleged child molesters accused of decades-old abuse. But on a 5-4 vote, the justices ruled unconstitutional this provision of the state's penal code that extended a statute of limitations for child molestation, allowing for prosecutions long after the crimes had allegedly occurred.

The two remaining criminal charges stemmed from evidence uncovered by the Truckee Police Department involving the molestation of the girl in 1995. Although Kiesle is believed to have molested scores of children over the years, the Tahoe Donner case is the one that finally brought him down. On May 16, 2002—a year before the Supreme Court decision that would have prevented prosecutors from trying the case—he was taken into custody and charged on one felony count of child molestation involving a girl under the age of fourteen.

Just as in his 1978 arrest, Kiesle pleaded no contest and was convicted. But this time, the law had some teeth. Kiesle, in 2004, was sentenced in Nevada County (California) Superior Court to six years in state prison. In addition, it was ruled he would be placed on parole for three years after his release from prison, would pay fines totaling $2,670, and would be required to give blood and fingerprint samples for law enforcement identification analysis. Finally, he would have to register as a sex offender for the rest of his life.

For the first time since 1968, when Kiesle is believed to have claimed his first victim, he would pay an actual price for what he'd done. Not that

I knew about any of this at the time; in fact, I wouldn't hear anything about Kiesle's status for another six years. His 2004 arrest and conviction made news in Northern California but why would anyone think of notifying me? Why would anyone think I'd be interested? Nobody but me and Robbie knew of my connection to the man—and I'd lost touch with Robbie soon after leaving Pinole in 1977 as a kid.

That said, for the first time in *thirty-six years*, Kiesle would experience what his victims, including me, had experienced ever since he began abusing us: what prison is like. The prisons of the victims don't come with bars or handcuffs or foot shackles like Kiesle's would. Ours come with guilt and shame and anger, which impede our every move, our every joyful moment, our every instance when we finally think we've outrun the demons only to once again be dragged back into the darkness.

Our imprisonment comes with insecurities, with fear of intimacy, with constant thoughts that we are forever tainted. Ours comes with dark nights in which we wonder if morning will ever come, with evenings in which soon after dinner we're already worrying about how we're going to sleep. Ours comes with flashbacks that jolt us from some pleasant experience into the filth of submitting to a selfish shell of a man, the candles on our daughter's birthday cake suddenly reminding me of how he'd light a candle in the rectory. And, just like that, we are robbed of experiences that should be pure joy. As if the sexual abuse alone weren't exploitation enough, its repercussions repeat, like the loop of a TV cartoon background. The *knowing*. The simple *knowing*. That is our prison.

I was among the lucky ones. I didn't commit suicide. A 2019 study (Thompson, Kingree, & Lamis) found child sexual abuse increased the risk by 1.4 to 2.7 times for "suicidal ideation" and "suicide attempts" in adulthood. Trauma in childhood, including sexual abuse, is highly correlated to depression, anxiety, alcohol and drug misuse, and earlier death (Merrick, Ford, Ports, & Guinn, 2018). But, again, I was fortunate.

I didn't get messed up in drugs. I didn't find it impossible to hold down a job. I didn't find it impossible to function within the framework of a family. Instead, I had a great mother, father, and sister. I helped start a family—we welcomed a daughter, Danielle, September 16, 2002—that, for now, wasn't perfect but seemed to be working. I cherished my two children. I enjoyed—and was good at—my job. I was surrounded by people who seemed to think I was OK.

And yet a layer of misery cut through my soul like a jagged knife. I paid the price. Those around me paid the price. A.J.: *Why does Daddy always fall asleep on the couch instead of going to bed?* Eileen: *Why doesn't Jim ever tell me how he really feels instead of pretending everything's great?* Work colleagues: *Why does Bartko obsess about always making everyone so damn happy? He's like a friggin' "must-please" machine with no power-off button.*

All of which is why, years later, when I finally heard, in 2010, about Kiesle being sentenced, I felt the deepest gratitude, and admiration, for the woman who had come forward. She refused to stay silent. And because of her courage a man who almost certainly would have struck again went to prison, keeping children safer.

If only I could have been so brave.

Chapter 11

As the new millennium began, the Bartko home had become like Denver on a Eugene-to-New-York flight—a mere stopover. A hub where people arrived *at* and left *from* but seldom a place where anyone went to just *be*. Eileen and I were two on-the-go travelers, each of us jetting here and there, though seldom on the same flight.

Amid the craziness of overstuffed schedules, Eileen and I were blessed with the arrival of our daughter, Danielle, on September 16, 2002. By then A.J. was nearly six.

As Danielle grew from a baby to a little girl, I found myself coaching her and A.J.'s sports teams. I gave them rides to school—Catholic schools, by the way—with stops for hot chocolate on the way. Sat courtside with them at Duck basketball games. And, with Eileen, took them on vacations. They were the light of my life.

A.J. had a math-oriented mind; at age five, he'd be watching a football game and suddenly say, "Dad, the Ducks have to score and go for two to win."

In years to come, the pattern would extend to Danielle, who came to think of Oregon athletes as extended "big brothers." I served as a volunteer reader in the kids' classrooms, took them to games, the works. As a family, I bonded more naturally with the kids than I did with Eileen; we both worked hard, Eileen returning to her job at Shorewood after Danielle was born. Meanwhile, neither of us was "there" for each other as much as we should have been. But we soldiered on.

In hindsight, my dedication to work and my ghost from the past proved to be a deadly combination for my marriage. If keeping busy kept my mind off Kiesle, it also detracted me from giving Eileen the attention she needed. At home, tension abounded like static electricity.

At work, the dynamics were different but the results the same—a growing sense of dysfunction. In a restaurant, what the diners see is finely crafted food arriving on their plates, hot, attractively displayed, and usually pleasing to the palate. Unless the restaurant is really quiet, they don't hear what's going on in the kitchen: plates breaking, chefs arguing with waiters, the owner having it out with an employee who insists on bringing her dog to work.

Athletic departments aren't much different.

As the new millennium dawned, outwardly we were living the dream. With ESPN's Game Day in town in the fall of 2000, Oregon beat a UCLA team that was being talked of as a national title contender and the Ducks finished the season with an impressive win over heralded Texas in the Holiday Bowl.

In keeping with our spirit of risk-taking, Oregon started the 2001 season by putting an 80-by-100-foot billboard of quarterback Joey Harrington on a Manhattan high rise, promoting him for the Heisman Trophy, and finished the season with a decisive win over Colorado in the Fiesta Bowl. (Joey finished fourth in the Heisman running.)

In 2002, the newly expanded Autzen Stadium opened, increasing ticket revenues by $2 million a year. In 2003, the Ducks beat Michigan at home and made the cover of *Sports Illustrated:* "Rich, cool and 4-0" read the headline.

Part of that "cool" was state-of-the-art locker rooms at Autzen that amazed the recruits and rankled the old schoolers. The $3.2 million, two-story addition included sofas, sixty-inch plasma-screen TVs, computer plug-ins, and lock boxes for valuables. At the time, nobody in the country had anything like it.

Even Moos was acting like a school kid. "Hey, guess what?" he said in reference to recruits looking for a place to play football. "We'll put you on a billboard in Los Angeles or San Francisco or New York. We'll market you in ways no one imagined."

In basketball, coach Ernie Kent led the Ducks, in 2002, to their first conference championship since 1945, going through the regular season undefeated at home, and made the Elite Eight in the NCAA basketball tournament. We started talking about scrapping the aging Mac Court for a new arena that would be more appealing to recruits and allow male bathroom-goers to forego the embarrassment of being hip-to-hip at the urinal trough.

And, for all practical purposes, the athletic department reached its goal of becoming self-sufficient by 2004, an incredible milestone considering the dark days of the 1970s when the Ducks were so poor they stopped feeding the media pre-game meals.

Yes, outwardly, UO was soaring; the restaurant looked impressive. But in the kitchen, if dishes weren't flying, a cold war had broken out. The wait staff of one of the managers, women's basketball coach Jody Runge, had mutinied. The restaurant's chief financial backer, Phil Knight, wasn't talking to the manager, Bill Moos. And one of our key chefs, track and field coach Martin Smith, seemed to be ignoring the very traditions that had made the menu so appealing to customers.

Runge's case shouldn't have become the mess it did. I liked Jody; her coaching abilities were obvious. In 2001, when the story exploded in the press, she was already the winningest women's basketball coach in Oregon history and drawing the biggest crowds ever for women's basketball at Mac Court. But she could be ruthless with her players, which, of course, doesn't make her all that different from a lot of other coaches, most of them men. And she made it known she was unhappy about not getting optimum court time at Mac Court for practices.

As the teapot started to simmer, a group of eight players came to Moos and complained about Runge's treatment of them. She had, they said, embarrassed players with tirades in front of thousands of fans. Communicated with them poorly. And instigated them to "play angry."

Moos brought in a Kansas City firm to investigate. When it was over, he announced at a news conference that Runge had resigned, though it was clear this wasn't her idea.

I thought it was an overreaction on Moos's part. There might have been some latent bitterness in Bill because Jody had never been subtle about her sense that women's sports played second fiddle at UO. I thought he could have fired a shot across her bow to see if she might be more diplomatic with Moos and ease up on her demands of the players, some of whose parents were passionately coming to the defense of their daughters.

Instead, she was suddenly gone. I got along well with her, which is probably why she chose me to be the administrator to help clean out her office—after hours. I was off that day but showed up, helped her move, then went to dinner with her and her mom at Mazzi's, an Italian restaurant in southeast Eugene. The previous night, while playing Nerf hoops with A.J., he'd accidentally elbowed me in the face, and I had a fairly pronounced shiner. I'm sure more than one restaurant patron, seeing me with Jody after her ouster, wondered just how I'd gotten it.

Moos's eyebrows raised when I walked in the next morning.

"Not what you think," I said. "And no way I'm paying for the dinner. That was not my idea of a good time."

Neither was trying to get a decent night's sleep. The pattern was predictable, as routine as brushing my teeth. I'd go to bed early and sleep for maybe an hour. But if I heard even the slightest noise—Eileen coming to bed, one of the kids getting up, a distant siren—boom, I'd awaken. And my night was doomed.

I'd toss, turn, sweat, shake.

Jimmy, want to go to a Warriors game Friday night?

My heart would race.

Maybe Robbie could join us for another sleepover.

I'd look at the clock radio, hoping it would be 5 or 6 AM; instead it would be 12:45 AM.

"Quit fidgeting," Eileen would say.

I wish I could have. She assumed it was work; I knew otherwise.

At about 3 AM I'd get up, watch some SportsCenter, sip some Chardonnay to relax. Back to bed. I averaged about four hours of decent sleep, per night. Then it was back to the office the next morning, ready to fix whatever needed fixing.

IF RUNGE'S DEPARTURE had been like a sudden firefight, Moos and Knight were locked in a cold war. For the last few years there had been a gradual falling out between the two. Guess who became the peacemaker between them?

In 2003 I'd become associate athletic director for donor relations; Phil, technically, was my responsibility but I saw my dealings with him as nothing but a privilege. He and I were close, and I grieved for him in May 2004 when his son, Matthew, thirty-four, died in a scuba accident. Phil went quiet for a few weeks—I read he got more than 2,500 notes of condolences—then returned, as engaged as ever, though I know he still grieves over the loss of his son.

Meanwhile, my relationship with Moos went back to WSU; as an associate athletic director he'd given me my first real job in the athletic department world. I held him in high esteem. A lot of people did. He was decisive. He was honest. He was forthright. And since arriving at Oregon in 1996 he'd done an outstanding job, happily allowing Nike's creative folks to help rebrand the football program and doggedly seeing to it that Autzen was expanded. He had lots of supporters and handled the media well, even after a bunch of seats at Autzen got double-booked and a throng of Wisconsin fans felt as if they were all losers in a game of musical chairs. He was smooth. He was unflappable. But time would prove he had an Achilles heel.

With the stadium expansion done, we were poised to go full speed ahead with the new basketball arena, something that was ticketed to cost more than $200 million. Phil, perhaps still a bit stung from the WRC controversy or perhaps cooling on Moos, wasn't putting his cards on the table yet, nor were we pestering him to do so. (He ran on PST—Phil Standard Time—and I'd long ago learned to not mess with that.)

The first crack in the Moos-Knight mortar was an interview Moos did with a Seattle radio station in early 2004. Although he attended, played football for, and was an associate athletic director at Washington State, Bill's roots were in Seattle, where the Ducks' rivals were looking for a new AD. When asked by the interviewer if he'd consider applying for the University of Washington, Moos said he would.

The comment stunned, and raised some hackles with, Duck fans. At a UO booster event in Portland, Moos was roundly booed, whether in tongue-in-cheek jest (not likely) or wounded pride (more likely). Among those reported to have joined in, according to *The Oregonian,* was Phil Knight.

Then came the Martin Smith flap. Over the years, Oregon's once-proud track and field dominance had slowly dwindled, particularly in the middle- and long-distance races. Many supporters of the program blamed that on Smith. They didn't believe the former Wisconsin track and field coach—hired to take over for Bowerman-disciple Bill Del-linger—was proving to be a worthy Keeper of the Tradition. Right or wrong, the perception from many within UO's storied distance-running tradition was that Smith didn't particularly care about carrying on the legacy of the three Bills—Hayward, Bowerman, and Dellinger. The UO traditionalists wanted distance-race dominance, home meets, Track Town USA, and big national meets at Hayward Field. (All of which happened, in the end, in part because of what would transpire regarding the head-coaching position.)

Smith simply wanted a great track and field program, which, in itself, was fine but ignored the university's rich distance-running history.

As with Moos and his radio comments, Smith's downfall was underestimating the power of emotion and the pull of history when it comes to supporters of college athletics, at least at Oregon. Like some other of the nation's best prep runners, when long-distance phenom Galen Rupp was trying to decide where to go to school he was cool on Smith and Oregon. Many saw the Central Catholic (Portland) runner as having Steve Prefontaine-level potential and thought he had the times and charisma to help restore UO's distance-running tradition. But he was coached by ex-UO runner Alberto Salazar, who was having a hard time recommending his alma mater with Smith in command. A meeting between Knight and Smith regarding Rupp's status did nothing to break the logjam.

"Jimmy," Phil said, "meet me at Sunriver. We have to talk about this."

By this point, 2004, Knight and Smith's boss, Moos, weren't talking to each other. It had gotten that bad between them. For an athletic department to have its top donor not getting along with its top athletic administrator, was clearly bad news.

When I arrived at the Trout House at the Central Oregon resort, Phil was already there, alone, with a box of cranberries and two cocktails for each of us.

"The politics on this one is like the Reagan-Russian negotiations," said Phil as the Deschutes River rolled by behind him. "I have no idea what's going on."

Rupp wanted Oregon but didn't want Smith. As a compromise, there was talk of Salazar coming to Eugene a few days a week to coach Rupp; such private-coach allowances weren't uncommon among universities. But Smith didn't like that idea. To complicate things, Galen's family—rightfully so—wanted a say in the decision; they wanted what was best for Galen but honored the close relationships their son had with Alberto, who'd coached their son since he was young.

"Rupp's talking about going to University of Portland or going pro," said Phil. "If we lose that kid when he wants to come here, it's a disaster. I mean, he can help change track and field, not just at Oregon but USA Track & Field. And we have a chance to bring the Olympic Trials here in 2008."

Some have suggested Knight used his leverage to oust Martin. Not true. Nobody did more than Knight to try to make things work with Martin. It was Knight who suggested bringing in a mediator—an out-of-state mediator—to see if some sort of reset button could be pushed. He actively looked for compromises that would allow Smith to stay.

Though Knight had started to doubt whether Moos was still the AD we needed, Phil's willingness to try to compromise suggests he hadn't completely given up on the guy. In terms of track and field, Phil just wanted to find ways to preserve the traditional "old Oregon way" while ushering in the new Oregon way. He was convinced both could work.

Ultimately, Martin refused to participate in the mediation, saying there was a conflict of interest with the people who chose the mediator—former Duck runners and Knight.

For Moos, the smart play seemed obvious: ask Martin to resign. And Moos initially seemed good with that. Instead, he stunned everyone by saying he wanted to give Martin a four-year extension. UO's track and field inner circle, Knight among them, wasn't happy.

The backlash, I think, surprised Moos. He realized this was strike two against him: the pro-Husky-job remark and now his backing of a guy who seemed indifferent to Oregon's strong running tradition. Perhaps realizing his own misstep, Moos reversed field and, in March 2005, asked for Martin's resignation. Smith was out.

"I'm looking for someone who appreciates the tradition and legacy of track and field at Oregon," Moos told *The Oregonian* in announcing that Martin was leaving.

It sounded great. UO hired former Stanford coach Vin Lananna as men's track and field coach and director of track and field and cross-country for both men and women. Lananna proved to be just what people thought he could be—among the finest coaches in the country and someone with great appreciation for the UO traditions of the past and great vision for track and field of the future. As for me—ever the pleaser, ever the "can't-we-all-just-get-along" guy—I was hoping Bill's about-face would help us recalibrate the program. Galen Rupp would enroll at Oregon and go on to Olympic greatness, we'd all kick back with a few drinks, and peace would again return to Duckville.

I was wrong. Moos's reversal didn't win him back the favor of Knight. Beyond passing remarks, the two hadn't talked regularly now for two years.

Enough. I set up a peace summit in Portland and encouraged both to attend. Just the three of us—at a conference room at Nike. Before they arrived, I'd set up a display of uniforms, bowl rings, trophies, all sorts of memorabilia that showed what Oregon athletics had accomplished since Moos arrived in 1996, a couple of years after me.

"Guys, look at this, look at all you've helped this university do in the last eight years," I began. "It's amazing. It's stuff we can all be proud of."

Though I noted an ever-so-slight melting of the ice, neither said a thing. Powerful men are tough to read sometimes because they tend to think to show emotion constitutes weakness. I needed to bore deeper, even if it was going to make me feel like a father whose two sons had been wailing away at each other in the backyard.

"I have to be honest, I'm tired of being stuck in the middle of this cold war. Phil, all these great accomplishments happened on Bill's watch; he's done a good job. Bill, I've never heard Phil once badmouth you behind your back."

Stone faces, both of them. Did they think I was crazy? I took a deep breath and continued.

"Bill, was Phil disappointed with the Husky comment? Yeah. Was he disappointed that you wanted to extend Smith's contract? Yeah; it was a slap in the face. But, guys, we've got to let bygones be bygones, trust each other, and move on. Because this setup ain't working. Not at all. And if something doesn't change, we all lose. Oregon, you guys, me, all of us."

I'd done my best to try to get Knight and Moos to re-engage with each other, but it wasn't happening. Moos, I think, always felt I sided with Knight, which was interesting since he's the one who stopped talking to Phil. If I was truly siding with Knight, wouldn't I be reveling in their communication gap? Wouldn't I be fueling their discord, instead of trying to broker peace between them? Wouldn't I perhaps be positioning myself for Bill's ouster so I could take over as AD?

As a sports fan dating back to roughly my first breath, I loved a game in which the underdog finds a way to win. Alas, this wouldn't prove to be such a game. My summit bought us some time as a staff—there was a slight thaw between the two and a few words spoken—but, ultimately, the Phil-Bill discord proved too much.

Both were brilliant men. Both cast wide shadows. Together, as my nifty table display showed, they helped Oregon athletics climb to a new level on the mountain. But it was like one of those old Western movies where one of the two cowboys says, "This town ain't big enough for the both of us." As the WRC controversy showed, Phil wasn't averse to leaving town if he felt it necessary. But this time he wasn't going anywhere. Moos was.

And as the year 2006 deepened, so, it turned out, was I.

Chapter 12

The previous few years at Oregon had been so splintered with friction that when the University of California-Berkeley approached me about a senior associate athletic director's job in 2006, I not only listened, I took it. I knew Cal had challenges of its own—foremost among them the need to upgrade a football stadium sitting on an earthquake fault line—but I was ready for a new challenge, too. And the Bay Area represented a "coming home" of sorts, though I quickly discovered that represented a double-edged sword.

I realized as much on my first trip to Berkeley, from the airport, across the San Francisco-Oakland Bay Bridge. I was on my way to begin a new life—Eileen and the kids, ages ten and five, were coming in six months—when the panic attack hit. Since 1973, I'd been racked with all sorts of emotional turmoil because of the abuse, but this was different.

This was like nothing I'd ever experienced.

My hands clutched the steering wheel of the rental car in a death grip. I froze like *Oz's* tin man without any oil. My mouth grew dry. My skin got clammy. My heart raced.

In retrospect, I realize part of it was simply the physical setup; I was driving sixty miles per hour over a massive body of water on an I-80 bridge for which there was no exit. I wanted to pull over but there was no room to do so. The inexorable moving forward with seemingly no choice intensified my panic. It was like being on some roller coaster that, soon after it jets forward, you regret having gotten on but realize it's too late to turn back.

Part of it, too, was that I was already second-guessing my decision to leave Oregon and come to Cal. I was familiar with the Bay Area—I'd grown up here and been back dozens of times—but the place seemed monstrous to me on this morning. Housing developments and high-rises seemingly stretched as far as I could see. Traffic was thick. What the hell was I doing here? What had I gotten myself and my family into?

And part of it, frankly, was *him*. As I headed north, passing Treasure Island, I knew that beyond Berkeley lay Pinole, about fifteen miles away. I assumed that Kiesle was living out there somewhere. After he went to prison in 2004 for six years, nobody had informed me that he'd been locked up because nobody knew I'd been one of his victims. (Of course, Robbie knew—Kiesle was his stepfather—but we hadn't spoken to each other since our childhood days and wouldn't reconnect for another decade.) Thus, all along, I had assumed Kiesle was a free man, since he'd never been given prison time for his 1978 conviction.

It wasn't that I feared he would hurt me again; I was a grown man. The power imbalance that enabled him to have his way with me and scores of children over nearly forty years was gone. No, it was just knowing he was *there*.

The meltdown was so massive that I seriously considered stopping. There was, of course, no place to pull over, so as with my life itself, I was forced forward more by the inexorable surge of those behind me than by any desire on my part. It wasn't that I didn't want the job at Cal, it was that my unresolved trauma from the past constantly reminded me that what I desired didn't really matter. My personal history would push and prod me as it pleased. In the end, the pain, the perpetrator, the past batted last. And I was powerless to do anything about it, short of pulling over and jumping over the side of the bridge.

I managed to get to my hotel—the elevator didn't help my sense of dread—and entered my room. I fell flat on my face on the floor, shaking like a man who'd just been hit by lightning. I was hyperventilating. I found that plastic liner for the ice bucket and tried breathing into it. Maybe it was psychological, but it seemed to help. I gradually calmed down.

Later, when I joined my first staff meeting, the warm welcome put me totally at ease. The people at Cal were awesome; glad to have me on board. But every few nights, in my hotel room, I'd find myself shaking again, gasping for breath. I needed sleep. I needed to be ready to face the next day. So, I'd open a bottle of wine, pour a glass, and sip—at, say, 3:15 AM.

Despite the almost daily pain, I had never seriously considered taking my life. But there were numerous nights when I wondered if I could go on. One morning I awoke in the hotel after another fitful night. As day broke, I could see it in the mist from my hotel—Alcatraz. There I stood, miles away, in the plushness of a Double Tree, imprisoned alone on my very own island of grief.

SIX MONTHS AFTER I'd left Eugene, Bill Moos resigned as AD, ushered out by a severance package. He'd done great things at Oregon and I wished him well. I was thrilled to see him reinvigorate football at my alma mater, Washington State, hoped he'd turn things around at Nebraska, and fervently believed he'd one day be inducted into the University of Oregon's Hall of Fame.

Meanwhile, as much as I enjoyed the people at Cal, it wasn't the fresh start I'd been hoping for, not even after Eileen and the kids joined me and we leased a house in Lafayette in the summer of 2006. To revive donor interest in Cal football, we desperately needed a new stadium, partly because it was old (built in 1923) and partly because it had been determined that the Hayward Fault passed directly beneath the playing field (just our luck). Building inspectors had recently said the stadium represented an "appreciable life hazard" in the event of an earthquake.

The stadium sat in a gorgeous setting called Strawberry Canyon, but aesthetics wasn't the problem. The problem was the money to renovate Memorial Stadium and add a student-athlete training center to it. The two projects initially were projected to cost about $140 million but ballooned to just under $500 million after years of delays caused by protesters—trees had to be cut down—and seismic fixes we had planned proved more expensive than originally thought.

The stadium obstacle sucked so much time, energy, and money from the athletic department that there was hardly any of the three left for other programs. When I took the job, I underestimated what a millstone around our necks the renovation was going to be. On top of our challenge of redoing a stadium while still needing to practice and play games—and of raising half a billion dollars to fund it—tree-sitters began protesting the removal of a grove of oaks to make room for the training center. For nearly two years—December 2006 to September 2008—the Save the Oaks Foundation held a tree sit-in. Apparently, it was—again, just our luck—the longest urban tree sit-in in history. And, despite my penchant for peacemaking, this time I saw no practical way to mediate this battle.

After Moos left Oregon, the new athletic director, Pat Kilkenny, called to see if I'd be willing to come back and fill the void. With Eileen's approval, I said yes. I'd been at Cal for just over a year. I regret I didn't give Cal what it needed; I hate letting people down. Above all, I regret putting my family through an abrupt move from Eugene and then, just when they were settling in and making friends, an abrupt move back. In particular, A.J., then ten, was angry—and I couldn't blame him. He'd just gotten settled in after being uprooted; now it was happening again. I felt terrible that A.J. had been wounded by my decision.

When he first heard the news, he went ballistic. He rushed into his room, slammed the door, and started ripping every Duck jersey, sweatshirt, and hat out of his drawers and closet in anger. When I finally managed to enter, he calmed down.

"I'm sorry, A.J.," I said. "I didn't mean to hurt you."

He sobbed, then spoke words that I could relate to, though for entirely different reasons.

"You're not hurting me on the outside," he said. "You're hurting me on the inside."

We hugged.

"Dad," he said, "can we just go watch SportsCenter together?"

It was among the most painful and heartwarming moments I'd ever spent with my son. His pain was my pain. I knew what it was like to hurt on the inside, too, even if nobody else knew that about me.

Back in Eugene, the University of Oregon was still on the rise. I hit the ground running. In August 2007, I helped organize the event at Nike at which Phil and Penny Knight announced their $100 million gift for the arena to be named in honor of their late son, Matthew. A groundbreaking ceremony was held February 7, 2009, and the $227 million arena opened just under two years later, January 2011.

Despite having given UO thirteen years, taken the Ducks to five NCAA tournaments, and twice making the Elite Eight, Ernie Kent wouldn't be around to coach basketball in the new arena. I felt bad about that; I liked Ernie. But sports are a fickle stage on which to ply one's craft.

It didn't help his case that, in 2005, he was unable to land either of two rare in-state standouts—Lake Oswego's Kevin Love or South Medford's Kyle Singler, who chose, instead, UCLA and Duke, respectively. It didn't help that certain matters regarding his personal life became public. But what sealed his fate was winning only twenty-four games in the previous two years.

I thought the world of Kent, but if his leaving was sad it was also inevitable. Even an idealist like me had come to understand that college athletics comes down to wins, losses, attendance, and donations.

People complain about how much money college coaches make. And without context, I get it. If I'm working my tail off teaching biology and learn that a linebacker coach made more last year in bowl-game bonuses than I make in a year, it hurts. But most assistant coaches have one-year contracts, and none enjoys the stability of tenure that many professors do.

Meanwhile, university presidents are among the smartest people around, otherwise they wouldn't be university presidents. If they truly didn't see a connection between athletics benefitting academics—one's success helping the other's success—they'd downscale athletics, lower coaches' pay, maybe even cut individual sports or entire programs altogether. But the reason they usually don't is because, as I said, they're smart. They're discerning. They know that it's awesome when the light goes on for some poli-sci major. That's a victory. That's what education is all about. That's *why we do this.* But they also know that, even with a good public relations staff like Oregon's, few of the school's alums are going to hear about this success. And, thus, aren't going to be inspired to begin donating money or increase their amount if they already are. Nor are high school students looking for a school going to be similarly inspired.

But on Saturday afternoon, when a Duck alum or a college-seeking student sees ESPN lauding Dennis Dixon's Statue of Liberty play that bamboozled Michigan, that alum is going to be more likely to give to the university—or, if a student, more likely to *attend* the university—than if the Ducks had lost 62-zip. Is that fair? Maybe, maybe not. But that's reality.

That reality doesn't mean students who play football are better than students who don't, or that football coaches are better than general faculty. It just means accepting the donor-driven reality that the accomplishments of student-athletes and coaches in the football program are more visible and have more potential to benefit the university financially.

Likewise, of course, it means that if a tenured geography prof has a couple of "off years" or engages in some personal indiscretions, that teacher isn't likely to get canned. The firing of Kent was yet another reminder that coaching on the Division I level is a high-risk stock. When you make the Elite Eight, win conference championships, and the like, you get bonuses atop your already-zero-heavy salary. People buy your dinner at Beppe & Gianni's Trattoria. You're all the rage on Twitter. But when you lose, you lose big. You can argue until you're blue in the face about whether it's fair, but that's the way college athletics work.

Not too long after I returned from Cal to UO in 2007, two things happened, one of which buoyed my sense of self-worth, the other of which shook me to my core.

The former was an offer from the University of Portland to become its athletic director. Portland, which had no football program, played in the West Coast Conference. It had a solid men's basketball program and one of the best women's soccer programs in the nation. It was a Catholic school. I was Catholic. They'd seen what we'd done at Oregon and, I think, believed I could bring some of that imagination to Portland.

I decided to pursue it. A.J. had two more years of high school left; Danielle was in elementary school. The plan was for Eileen—no longer working outside the home—and the kids to stay in Eugene while A.J. finished high school. Deep down, I suppose I thought letting A.J. finish out his high school years was something of a makeup call for the disastrous Eugene-Berkeley-Eugene moves I'd initiated—and quiet affirmation for my choosing to stay put when I was his age and my folks moved from Modesto to Spokane.

The process was not long and drawn-out. In fact, on the night before I was to go in for my second interview, the president called me and flatout offered me the job. The salary was good. I had twenty-four hours to decide.

"It's yours, Jimmy," said Father William Beauchamp. "We can announce it tomorrow. What do you think? We'd love to have you here at Portland."

It felt good to be wanted. It wasn't like I felt unappreciated at Oregon. But when you've been in a job for nearly twenty years—despite my brief stint at Cal—the rut of routine dulls that sense of appreciation. I'd been part of an incredible ride, watching a program that had been in two bowl games in the previous thirty years make seventeen such postseason events since I'd arrived. I'd had the privilege of working with an amazing group of truly generous donors, most of whom weren't interested in taking any credit. But I also had blurred the line between work and home, worn myself down to the point of getting sick, and found myself in too many "pissing matches" with people who thought they'd been promised a skybox on the fifty-yard-line and were mad that they only got the forty-seven.

This was fresh. This was new. This was me getting to run my own show.

But I turned it down.

Why? My "reason of record" would be that I panicked. For the first time in my administrative career, I made a decision before I was comfortable making it. For some reason the president wanted to sew up the deal right then and there. I should have politely asked for a few days to consult more with Eileen, talk to a few more people, pray a little. Instead I just told him no. Sorry, but no. It just didn't feel right. The timing wasn't right. Yes, I've reminded myself over and over since then—with a touch of latent anger: the reason I didn't take the job was all about timing. No time to think it through. A rushed process.

Or was the real reason this—that when I imagined daily life on a campus with priests, chapels, and candles, I worried it could trigger too many flashbacks and unloose more trauma.

I regret saying no to the University of Portland—although plenty would happen in subsequent years that I would regret far more. Regardless of the outcome, the process had been a pleasant shot of affirmation for me, and I needed that.

The second thing that happened, the one that shook me to my core, happened in a different place at a different time about a different matter. In January 2010, I flew to Berkeley to watch a Cal-Oregon basketball game, one of the worst losses—87-59—the Ducks would suffer in years. The next morning, at the Claremont Hotel's Paragon Restaurant, I was having coffee and leafing through the *Oakland Tribune* when I saw a headline that sent shivers through me like an electric shock: "Priest Who Abused Children Released from Prison."

It was him. Kiesle. No longer the mid-twenties young man who'd abused me, instead, the sixty-two-year-old man who'd abused me. Bearded. Old. Sad. The sight of him in the mug shot repulsed me. Slowly, with no thought to what I was doing, I bent over and lay my forehead on the table.

"Sir, are you all right?" asked a waiter.

"Uh, yeah," I said, sitting up again. "Just some unexpected news."

I started to get a flash of symptoms like I'd experienced that time on the I-80 bridge. Panic. Thirty-eight years after he sexually abused me, I was, for the first time, looking at the face of the man who scarred me, and many others, for life. As I read the story I learned, for the first time, that there'd been others besides Robbie and me. Scores of others. We weren't alone. I wasn't alone. It was partly affirming and partly sickening.

Frankly, I hadn't spent much time in the last four decades wondering what had happened to Kiesle, wondering whether he was a free man or wound up in prison. But what did it matter now? Though a registered sex offender, he was living with his wife—my friend Robbie's mother—in a gated community in plush Walnut Creek. By now, Robbie had told his mother that he had been one of Kiesle's victims. Though he said she expressed regret, she also quickly rationalized her husband's acts by saying he'd been abused himself in seminary.

The news of Kiesle having been released from prison made me feel like vomiting. It was too overpowering. The room spun. The story so rattled me I almost missed my flight back to Eugene. All the way home, I wrestled with what this meant to me. What *should* it mean to me? Do I pretend I never saw it? That was my default format; that's what I'd done for nearly forty years. Pretend the most defining moments of my life had never happened. And now the monster was threatening to get loose. Did I want that or not?

By the time I got home, I'd made my decision. I walked in. Eileen was already in bed. I showed her the newspaper article, hoping it would provoke some response—some encouragement, some concern—that might lead to my opening up about the abuse.

"Please read it and let me know what you think," I said.

She took the newspaper into her hands, puzzled.

I wanted to tell her that I was one of those kids. Finally, I was ready. I went downstairs, giving her time to read it. When I returned, she was asleep, the paper on the floor, crumpled as if she'd simply tossed it aside.

In retrospect, I should have told Eileen the context behind the article—that I'd been one of the victims. But that was easier said than done. Once you've kept a secret for a lifetime, it isn't easy letting it go. My intent with the newspaper article was a sort of foot-in-the-door attempt to trigger some interest on her part. What I wanted her to say was: "Jim, what's going on? Why did you give me this? Oh, my God, were you—?" That's obviously not the response I got.

Shame on me for not having the guts to simply say what needed saying. But, oh, how I wish she'd offered me even the slightest affirmation I was so desperately seeking. Why had she apparently ignored the article? Was she in denial—suspecting that I could have been a victim but not wanting confirmation because the answer might be yes? Or did she simply not care if there was a connection between the man in the newspaper story and me?

I should have told her about the abuse when we first started getting serious with each other, but I feared she'd consider me damaged goods and I'd lose her. Ironically, in the end, a similar scenario would play out in our relationship. Meanwhile, the wild roller-coaster ride for UO athletics would at least temporarily divert my attention from a marriage that, if not on the brink of collapse, was starting to feel serious stress.

Chapter 13

The winds of change were blowing in the UO athletic department, though nothing like the full-scale hurricane I would experience myself down the road.

In March 2009, Oregon announced that Mike Bellotti—the winningest football coach in UO history—was stepping down and would be replaced by Chip Kelly. The previous fall the Ducks had gone 9-3, beaten Oregon State 65-38 to keep the Beavers out of the Rose Bowl, and downed thirteenth-ranked Oklahoma State in the Holiday Bowl. A great season. But Bellotti was fifty-eight and the dean of Pac-12 coaches. Because of his busy schedule, he'd seen only a few of his youngest son Sean's high school football games. And Kelly, the offensive coordinator Bellotti had hired the previous year, was turning heads with a no-huddle offense that was among the nation's best. The previous December,

Kelly had been designated as the school's "coach in waiting"—Bellotti's replacement when he chose to step down—and now Mike felt it was time. Though administration wasn't his passion, he agreed to take over as athletic director for Kilkenny, whose original agreement was to stay for two years.

In 2009, Kelly's career at Oregon—and Bellotti's stint as AD—started out with a nightmarish 19-8 road loss to Boise State, after which a frustrated Duck running back, LeGarrette Blount, slugged a BSU player in the face on national TV. Had there ever been a lower moment for Oregon football in the modern era? But what followed was the most remarkable comeback season I've ever seen. Oregon won ten straight games to make the Rose Bowl, won the Pac-12 championship, twice was featured on ESPN's *Game Day*, and embarrassed USC 47-20 on Halloween in what many will remember as Kelly's "here-I-am-world" game. It was one of the worst losses in USC history, afterward coach Pete Carroll calling his team "a mess."

Kelly proved to be a masterful hire as head coach. Defenses didn't know what to do with his hurry-up offense; some faked injuries to get timeouts so they could catch their breaths. But few could keep pace with Oregon—in points or in the innovation of uniforms and helmets. On October 27, 2010, a University of Oregon football team, for the first time since the school started playing football in 1894, was voted by the Associated Press as the No. 1 football team in the country. That, of course, is not a national title bestowed at the end of the year or earned in one of the championship games that began in 2008. Still, for at least that week—and many weeks to come—UO stood atop the football mountaintop.

The Ducks won an unprecedented twelve games—I still remember the "12-0" T-shirts—and suddenly found themselves at a place where Phil Knight always thought we could be, even if I wasn't quite as confident: playing for a national championship. In January 2011, in Glendale, Arizona, we played Auburn tooth-and-nail but lost 22-19.

I didn't have time to wallow in defeat. Three days later Matthew Knight Arena was making its debut with a Thursday night game against USC; we had only seventy-two hours to get final approval from the city of Eugene, make sure the scoreboard worked, and teach the Duck mascot to descend on a swing from the ceiling of the building. Thanks to extraordinary efforts from Nike's Mike Doherty, we made it work.

But once that happened—all went well, including our winning the game—I finally had a chance to put our football program in perspective. In a little over a decade, Oregon had become to college football what the Dallas Cowboys had become to the NFL: America's team. Perhaps initially intrigued by the Joey ("Heisman") Harrington billboard, college sports fans in New York were buying more gear from the Duck Store in Eugene online than people from any other state except Oregon, Washington, California, and Texas. In Northern California, the Ducks were, in terms of merchandise, more popular than Stanford. In 2014 Florida State won college football's national championship but Oregon made $200,000 more than the Seminoles in merchandising royalties. And the next season UO beat the Seminoles 59-20 in the Rose Bowl to qualify for yet another national championship game.

Donations rocketed to a record high. Enrollment from out-of-state students, particularly those from California, shot up, and international students enrolled at UO at unprecedented rates, many of them arriving well-versed in how to put their fingers together to "flash the O." (A hand gesture, by the way, that Joey Harrington had started in 2001.) One Saturday morning, a carload of Utah State students—yes, students from a faraway school—showed up in Eugene after an all-night drive—734 miles—just to experience a Duck game at Autzen Stadium. In short, Duck football had risen to unprecedented levels of popularity.

For me, UO's success shouted, "mission accomplished." No matter what happened in the future, we'd done it. Somehow—through risk-taking, creativity, great coaching, amazing athletes, shrewd marketing, and millions of dollars from donors—Oregon had risen to the top echelon of college football, and academics had benefitted handsomely from the ascension.

It felt good.

But, personally, it also felt like time for a new adventure. When Fresno State, near the end of 2014, asked me to apply for its just-opened athletic director's job, I did so, with Eileen's blessing. By now A.J. was preparing for college at Loyola Marymont in Los Angeles and Danielle was going to be a sixth-grader at O'Hare Elementary in Eugene. Of the two kids, it was her life that would be most disrupted.

On the day I learned about Fresno State's interest in me, I turned to her. "What do you think, Danielle. Should I try for this job?"

"You'd be a great AD, Dad," she told me. "Sure."

Her response melted my heart. At twelve, she had already filled my life with inspiration, not the least of which had come when Duck basketball player Carlos Emory didn't have any family to walk him to center court on Senior Day. We'd often have players over for dinner and some invariably became "family." Danielle always "adopted" a favorite basketball player each year; in 2013, Carlos was her guy. She happily stepped up and walked him to center court—a fifth-grader!—while many in the stands, especially yours truly, wiped away tears. He called her his "favorite little sister."

I knew a little bit about Fresno State. It was a member of the Mountain West Conference, had an enrollment of about 25,000 students—similar to Oregon's—and had a football program that had had only two losing seasons since 2000, though the current one was becoming its third. Fresno State's coach, Tim DeRuyter, was a tough-as-nails former Air Force player who had a reputation for turning so-so defenses into stone walls. But after back-to-back conference titles with future NFL quarterback Derek Carr at the helm, the Bulldogs were struggling through what would be a 6-8 record in a rare fourteen-game season. Attendance was down. Grumbling among fans was up.

The football stadium, which seated 41,031, was a disaster; it needed a huge upgrade. The fan support was solid among the older generation but slipping beyond that. Fresno State desperately needed a return to the glory days of the 1980s and early '90s, when, under coach Pat Hill and previously Jim Sweeney, it was beating the likes of Wisconsin, UCLA, Georgia Tech, Washington, Oregon State, and Kansas State, and often ranked among the nation's Top 25.

I looked at the school as something of a sleeping giant. It had once been one of those smaller Division I schools that could run with the big boys—"We'll play anybody, anywhere, anytime," Hill had once crowed, with the wins to back him up—and I was eager to help the school return to such grandeur.

The interview process was far more extensive than the one I'd had with the University of Portland. A search firm arranged to have me meet with its representative for dinner in Portland, after which I learned I was a finalist. I flew to Los Angeles where, at an airport hotel, I gathered with the school's eighteen-person search committee. There were nine people on each side of the table; it looked like one of those "Last Supper" paintings. But if the setup initially looked intimidating, I felt comfortable once the questions began.

I was somewhat surprised when, amid more stock questions, someone asked, "How's your family taking this? After all, you have children in school. It's not easy uprooting a family."

"Put it this way," I said, "my daughter told me, 'Dad, you'd be a great AD.'"

I didn't know where such candor had come from—opening up about personal things in my life had never been a strength. And I didn't know where the sudden surge of emotion came from as I spoke—perhaps from too many long days and sleepless nights and blurred lines between work and family. But with that I promptly wiped away tears. My lips literally quivered; I could hardly talk.

Later, I wondered if that had been seen by the committee as a weakness—probably, I supposed—but I'd always thought the best approach in such matters was simply to be yourself. Be genuine. *What you see is what you get.* Except, of course, in matters where complete disclosure would hurt essentially everyone you loved and hoped to protect from the same pain you'd been through. That's why, even after learning about Kiesle being released and showing Eileen the article, I continued to hold onto The Secret like some football coaches tell their running backs to hold onto the ball: *You fumble, the ball explodes, and you and your teammates die. Get it? Hold on to the friggin' ball!*

After LA, I flew to San Francisco to interview with the president of the school, Joseph Castro, and the head of the search committee. A few years younger than me, Castro had earned his undergraduate degree from Cal and graduate degree from Stanford. He was a former dean of students in Berkeley. Married. Kids roughly my kids' ages. Not a rabid sports fan, it seemed, but one of those presidents who understood the necessity of athletics to help a school like this. I liked him. As we talked, my respect for him deepened, even if we didn't agree on every aspect of the direction of the athletic program.

He told me a little bit about his perspective on athletics and academics; nothing out of the ordinary until he expressed his desire to bring back wrestling and women's water polo, both having been cut for financial reasons years ago. In this day and age, adding sports was not the default format; saving existing programs was. Oregon, for example, had dropped its wrestling program to help balance the number of women's sports with men's sports, as required by Title IX. Fresno State had a pool and locker room for women's water polo but would need to add a facility for men's wrestling.

"What do you think about that?" he asked.

I knew that Fresno State, about a decade before, had come under extreme fire from at least three female administrators and coaches who ultimately won lawsuits against the school for sexual discrimination—about $30 million worth in lost lawsuits. I knew that a judge had described what he saw as a "generally demeaning atmosphere tolerated and even fostered" by sports administrators toward women. And I knew that, though the backlash hadn't happened on Castro's watch—he only arrived the year before I did—the university needed to be diligent in providing equal opportunities for women.

"Tough time to be adding sports, what with Title IX," I said. "And I'd be a little worried about the added financial burden. These aren't revenue-producing sports."

"Not so sure about that," he said. "I think together they could produce half a million dollars."

His answer didn't jibe with the reality of college sports or in the report on my desk in Eugene after a three-month study by an outside firm. Sounded like wishful thinking to me. Football was always the financial engine that pulled the other programs. At Fresno State, which was experiencing dwindling attendance and had a dilapidated stadium that needed a major overhaul, the only way to make money was to invest money.

At some major universities, basketball could earn its keep with a great season, though that was impossible at Fresno State because of an inane setup regarding the school's arena, the Save Mart Center. Not only did the contract require the athletic department to pay rent for what was, in essence, its own facility, but the department did not get profits from games, concerts—any events held in it; proceeds all went to a general fund.

All in all, the department's financial status looked precarious; for me, personally, this smacked of gambling my career on a high-risk stock.

"We could make it happen," I said. "Sure. We could add those sports."

The rest of the interview went great; I was impressed with Castro, with his warmth, knowledge, and commitment to the university. I flew home to Eugene, hoping I'd be offered the job and, a few days later, was thrilled that I had.

I said yes.

My leaving created an odd juxtaposition of emotions. Oregon was on the stretch run of its second national championship appearance in four years—this is what we had always strived for—and yet I was packing to leave for another job.

On January 12, 2015, in Dallas, I cheered on Oregon with wild abandon against Ohio State in the "Natty" but the Ducks, both of their lines badly outsized and outmatched, were never really in it. They lost, 42-20. And I moved on to Fresno State, my colleagues happy for me, Phil, in particular, excited to see what I could do with this opportunity.

"I have known and worked with Jim Bartko for twenty years," Phil said in a statement he released. "He has played a significant role in the growth and improvement of the University of Oregon athletic department. As an Oregon alum and contributor, I hate to see him go, but Fresno State has made a great hire."

There were a few misty eyes as I said my goodbyes, mine included, but that was the nature of the beast. People move on. And now it was my time.

I stepped into the unknown thinking I had nothing to lose—only to learn that I had much to lose.

And much, it turned out, to gain.

Chapter 14

He was a mid-level donor, mid-forties, and mad as hell. "I'm drop-ping my season tickets," he told me when I called on him, one of hundreds of donors I personally touched base with in my first months in Fresno.

"Now, hold on, Sam," I said. "Why would you do that?"

"I gave $5,000 last year and didn't hear from a soul. All I ever get is an automated e-mail telling me to renew."

I couldn't blame the guy. Donors don't need a parade thrown in their honor. They just want to feel appreciated—like they're part of some-thing. And, not to sound schmaltzy, but they just want to feel as if some-one cares about them. To some degree, isn't that all of us? To feel like we matter?

"Stay with us," I said. "That's going to change. See what our vision is.

Give me—give *us*—a year to prove that things are going to be different."

Sam renewed and donated another $5,000.

Relationships. That's where I immediately focused my attention when I arrived in Fresno. Just as in Medford nearly thirty years earlier, I started to meet the "who's who" of Bulldog donors with a blend of confidence and humility. Make necessary changes, sure. But first, listen. Learn. Lock into the cultural nuance and history instead of imposing "the Oregon way" on anybody. *Hey, I'm new around here. Help me understand this place.* That was a big part of my mantra.

The most important lesson I learned, early on, was that Fresno State had treated its older donors with great respect but was neglecting the next generation, the younger supporters we needed on board. We needed such people to catch some sort of vision that was greater than themselves—and help them understand that they could help make it happen.

Sports have this amazing ability to bring people together, this amazing power to draw a diverse gathering of fans for a common purpose, this amazing potential to bring out the best in us all. At times, I've wondered where I'd be without sports having not done the same for me on a personal level. They've been the catalyst for the richest relationships I have. They've been the challenge to stretch me for all I'm worth. And they've been the complement to academic programs at the two schools I'd worked for—Oregon and Cal.

With an eye toward fostering this kind of togetherness at Fresno State, I threw a dinner for forty-eight people, sat back, and listened. What I heard was the same thing the mid-forties fan had told me: Nobody had talked to them in ten years. I found all the attention was going to about two percent of the donors; the others felt neglected. That had to change. We needed buy-in from a far broader base, particularly the post-Baby Boom generation. We needed to upgrade a stadium that had crumbling seats, virtually no concession stands, and no elevators for people with disabilities.

In February 2015, I introduced AECOM, a design team that I had worked with at Oregon, to present conceptual illustrations for a renovated Bulldog Stadium. The buzz began. But football facilities weren't our only need. Our track and field program had no track. Our tennis courts had cracks that looked like a river's tributary system. And amid this, President Castro wanted to add two sports.

Relax, I told myself. Just when everything would seem overwhelming, I'd just keep repeating my mantra: *relationships.* And think, *find a way to add wrestling and water polo.* Those additions weren't my idea, but it was clear my boss wanted the sports and I would do my utmost to make them happen. I wanted to make him proud, wanted to show him that I wasn't at Fresno State to fatten my resume and move on, but to help create an athletic program that would reflect well on the university.

Fresno, I soon realized, had 500,000 people in and around it but still exuded a small-town feel. Everywhere I went, I'd find someone I'd just met a few weeks before. In my first year I tried to meet with every significant donor I could. I met with the media. I got to know some people with whom I'd be working, including Debbie Adishian-Astone, the interim vice president of administration who would soon lose the "interim" in her title, and Steve Robertello, the interim AD before I arrived and now my assistant.

"Bartko was a breath of fresh air and a bundle of energy," wrote Marek Warszawski in the *Fresno Bee.*

The feeling was mutual. I was loving the gig, the only downer being that Eileen and the kids were still in Oregon; they'd move down when Danielle was out of school in June. And, soon, A.J. would graduate and be off to Loyola Marymount in LA.

On May 13, roughly four months after my arrival, one of our top boosters asked me to meet him for dinner one evening. I walked into the restaurant and was puzzled to see so many people I knew—Fresno State coaches, donors, and administrators.

"Surprise!"

I looked around. There were Eileen, A.J., Danielle, and nearly eighty others whose common denominator was Fresno State. I was stunned. It was a surprise celebration for my fifty-first birthday, an event in which the university had flown my family down from Oregon to attend.

I couldn't remember the last time I'd felt so warmly affirmed. My tears said it all. That night I not only arrived home with nearly eighty bottles of wine—everyone brought one as a gift—but with a sense that this was a special place. These were special people. Givers—folks who reminded me of my Grandma Patricia, who, along with my mom, was my standard for living with others in mind.

Of all the coaches I'd met, my favorite, frankly, was our most important coach, at least when it came to financial sustainability: Tim DeRuyter, the football coach. When I arrived, Fresno State was coming off a 6-8 season. Clearly, we needed to do better than that. But in 2015 we were 3-9. It was just the opposite of what we needed. Fresno State's turnaround depended on a new surge of donor money, but donors shut down if they're not seeing progress. You don't have to have a stellar season every year, but you do need to show you're heading in that direction. We weren't. In fall of 2016, the Bulldogs started the season 1-7. Fans were restless.

What cast a personal awkwardness to the situation was that Eileen and I had become good friends with Tim and his wife, Kara, and their children. They made us feel like family. We'd dined together, played golf together. When Eileen and Danielle joined me in Fresno, one of the DeRuyter's daughters would babysit Danielle. They were just wonderful people, a grand addition to our lives. Which is why it was so hard when I realized a painful truth: I had to fire Tim.

It was, by far, the hardest thing I've ever done in this business. I hate to hurt people because I know what it's like to be hurt. But the losing wouldn't stop. In 2016, my second year at FSU, the Bulldogs were headed for the worst season in school history. The team's four wins in two years marked another all-time low. Whatever patience donors had clung to was gone; donations were drying up. The letters, e-mails, and text messages poured in daily. The common theme? The Bulldogs needed a new coach. I agreed. So did President Castro.

On October 23, 2016, when I broke the news to Tim in my office, his pain was my pain. I don't say that to elicit any sort of sympathy; he was the one who was going to be out of a job, not me. But now, nearly forty years into this business, I also knew that, although my "keep everyone

Jim Bartko collection

Jim Bartko collection

Top: Convict Lake, near Mammoth, California, has been my "happy place" since I was young. Above: At the lake with friends Roger Orth, Marvin Adams, and Olympic decathlete Roger George. I used to go to the lake to fish with my friends. Now, besides that, I also go to the lake in my mind ... to help block out painful memories of the past.

Rich Seow

Dave Frey

Top: Deep in thought, far right, at the 2008 U.S. Olympic Track & Field Trials at Haywad Field with, left to right, Vin Lananna, Oregon men's track and field coach and director of track and field and cross-country for both men and women; Phil Knight; and my great friends, Denny and Carey McNally, big supporters of UO athletics. Above: PTSD from child abuse, I've learned, is far darker than any loss on the track, field, or court.

In 2010, Kiesle was released from prison after serving six years in connection with the sexual molestation of a girl in Tahoe Donner, California. In Oakland, when, by chance, I saw the newspaper article about his release, it was the first I'd read about the man who'd abused me. I almost got physically sick.

Why did Fresno State AD Jim Bartko leave?
Divorce papers say he's battling alcoholism
fresnobee.com

Top: The early days at Fresno State had me smiling a lot. Middle: at a pep rally to fire up our Bulldogs basketball fans. Bottom: The story that broke the day after I separated from Fresno State.

Top: The family gathered near Mount Hood in Oregon for Thanksgiving 2018: left to right, my sister's husband Keith (with Marcus the dog), father Jim, sister Kim, daughter Danielle, son A.J. (with Ellie), and mother Mary Jane (with Stella). Left: In 2019, Robbie joined me for a Ducks game at Autzen Stadium. Because of what we went through together, he will always be a friend like no other.

Top: Stella, my new English Golden Retriever, has not only been a friend but the epitome of loyalty during my difficult times. Above: At a Garth Brooks concert at the University of Oregon's Autzen Stadium with two of my favorite people: my sister Kim, left, and daughter Danielle, summer of 2019.

happy" bent still ran strong, at times you had to make decisions for the greater good, decisions that hurt good people in the process. A dozen other coaches and their families were likely going to be upended if our new coach hired his own staff.

Tim, naturally, was crushed when I broke the news to him in my office, with Castro and Adishian-Astone looking on. He wanted more time to turn things around. But college athletics run a hurry-up offense. As I got up to leave, I hugged him. When he and the two others left, I buried my face in my hands. My eyes were wet with tears. I'd been in Fresno just over a year, and already had experienced the highest of highs, the surprise party, and the lowest of lows, having to fire a good man— and a good friend.

But every athletic director knows that if your football program isn't doing well, donor dollars fall and the number of empty seats at games rise. Each of those seats represents potential income for the university. And, if you wait too long, the engine expected to pull the entire athletic program—twenty-two sports, in our case—careens off the tracks and the entire train twists into unsalvageable carnage. It was my job to make sure that didn't happen.

I knew immediately who I wanted as our new coach: Jeff Tedford. Jeff, then fifty-five, had played football at Fresno State in the early '80s. He had been an assistant at Fresno State and Oregon before turning around an absolutely rancid Cal program in the early 2000s as head coach. A few years later Cal rose to the No. 2 ranking in the nation. And in 2011 Tedford became the winningest coach in the school's history.

The two of us had overlapped for five years at Oregon and for my year-and-a-half at Cal. I was confident we could get him. He'd coached for a handful of pro and college teams since being let go by Cal in 2011 after a two-year slide. And I knew Fresno State had a special place in his heart. Tedford was just like our mascot, a bulldog. Though happily married, he'd been known to sleep on an air-mattress overnight in his office from time to time. In that respect, and with his forte being offense, he reminded me a bit of Oregon's Chip Kelly, the hottest young football coach in the nation.

Though I agreed to look beyond Tedford—I wanted to prove he was the best we could get—I asked Castro for permission to run the search on my own. In my estimation, that was what they were paying me for: to help revive their athletic program and to trust me for my decisions. He agreed.

As my search intensified, so did my insomnia-anxiety combination, if it could get any worse. I wasn't stressed about the hire. I was sad about having to fire Tim. My survivor's guilt wouldn't go away. When a new coach arrives at a school, he usually brings in his own staff, so Tim's leaving would likely mean at least a dozen assistants leaving, too. Lying on the couch in the wee hours of the night, I'd do the math. I'd count the number of assistant coaches and their wives and kids whose fathers would be jobless because of my actions. The tally was somewhere north of fifty. *Their pain, my fault.*

On nights like that, when the face of Stephen Kiesle inevitably appeared in darkness, I would never say to myself, in relation to him: *Your pain, his fault.* I'd never really thought of it that way. More than forty years had passed, but my anguish was always about the guilt I felt for letting it happen to me. And for harboring The Secret, which deepened the guilt, which kept me awake, which made me less of a husband and father than I needed to be, which lowered my self-image, which returned me to The Secret, which deepened the guilt, which kept me awake … and it repeated, like one of those animated emojis, over and over.

"Come back to bed," Eileen would say at some ungodly hour of the night.

"In a minute," I'd say, then finish my last glass of wine with hopes I could at least get a few hours of sleep.

We posted the job for five days. Our five-person selection committee—Castro; Adishian-Astone; Dawn Lewis, faculty athletic rep; Brian Pannish, a donor; and Terry Donovan, the athletic chief financial officer—began sorting through resumes. Most had no idea how difficult turning around a football program could be, but having seen it done at Oregon and Cal, I knew it could be a long and arduous journey. We interviewed four finalists, all in a single day, flying in Brian's private plane from Fresno to Oakland and to Seattle, then back.

After completing the last interview, we went through our notes on the flight home. I knew Tedford needed to be our coach. Others weren't convinced. Some were concerned that the grades of Cal's football players had slipped while he was there. Others that he'd been out of coaching and, thus, wasn't deserving of what I wanted to pay. My plan was to offer him $1.55 million per year for five years; no increases. That was substantially less than what DeRuyter and other coaches in the conference were making. However, I wanted to build in lofty incentives that gave him the potential to be among the conference's best-paid coaches if he had great seasons.

Tedford wanted the job. He told me that he missed being a head coach and that there was something appealing about capping a coaching career at your alma mater. He'd been born and raised here. He still had connections in the community. And when I told him what an uphill battle this was going to be, he didn't cringe in the least. Instead, he seemed hungry for the challenge, pointing out that he'd contributed to Oregon's rags-to-riches story, and to Cal's turnaround.

Ultimately, the committee unanimously chose to back my decision to hire him, though, for a few, it was a tepid endorsement. We put the contract together with Jeff's agent, made minor adjustments, and the president and I both signed off on it. We still needed official approval from our athletic corporate board, which was usually a rubber-stamp exercise and, as such, would come after the next day's news conference.

On November 10, 2016, I walked to the podium, welcomed people, and announced Jeff as our new football coach. "I have faith that Jeff is just the ticket to bring back the winning tradition of Fresno State football," I told the few dozen people. "He will also be at the forefront of ushering in a new era with our Bulldog Stadium modernization project. I look forward to his leadership, on and off the field."

I prefaced my remarks by saying what made Jeff special had nothing to do with X's and O's, however. Instead, I said it was "first and foremost, integrity." I've always admired straight shooters, folks who were genuine, who, behind closed doors, are just as they are in public, be they coaches, college administrators, or priests.

The next week, by protocol and phone, I went before the fourteen-member "Athletic Corp Board" to get approval of our athletic budget, including the money for coaches. The "Tedford concrete," as it were, wouldn't be completely dry until the board signed off.

During the conference call, after I explained why Tedford was a great fit, I asked for comments and questions.

"Why do we need to pay him so much?" asked a board member. "He got a huge buyout at Cal."

"Yeah," said Adishian-Astone, "if he loves Fresno State so much, why doesn't he coach for free? Or at least give us a Fresno State discount because he's an alum."

Was she serious? Apparently so. I hadn't expected this. And the doubters weren't through.

"If he's so good, why isn't he a head coach now?" someone else asked.

The comment was so asinine, so petty, I didn't quite know how to respond.

But now the Tedford skeptics had some momentum. "I think we need someone younger and cheaper," said the president of the board.

"Jim Harbaugh at Michigan has a base salary of $100,000," said the board president.

"He's one of the top-paid coaches in the country," I said. "Universities pay coaches in an array of ways. Harbaugh is making over $10 million this year. We're offering Jeff a nice package that's incentive-heavy but it's not even a third of that. It doesn't hurt that Tedford's roots are right here. He's a former Bulldog. This is home. That'll mean something to our fans and donors."

"I'm sorry, Jim," said the board president, "but do you want Tedford because you know him, because you drank beer with him at Oregon, or because he'd be the best choice?"

I was surprised at the pushback. My familiarity with Tedford was shifting from asset to liability, as if the others thought this was shaping up to be a "good-ol'-boy" hire.

"I want Jeff because I think he gives Fresno State our best chance to return to greatness," I said.

"If he's so hot, why has he bumped around since getting the boot at Cal?" asked another board member.

I pointed out that Tedford's "bumping around" included being hired by the likes of Chris Petersen at Washington, one of the most highly respected college coaches in the nation; Lovie Smith, head coach of the Tampa Bay Buccaneers in the NFL; and the Canadian Football League's BC Lions, where he led the team to the playoffs.

"And before that he took a Cal team that had nineteen straight losses and not only stopped the streak but beat Washington and Stanford, and was named the Pac-12's Coach of the Year—in his first year."

"While much of his team was flunking out," someone chimed in.

"He breathed life back into a dead program," I said, "and that strengthened the entire university. For a decade, the team's academic record was outstanding except for the hiccup in the last year."

Finally, with far more resistance than I expected, the board officially approved Tedford's contract. Still, it was clear that some people thought my choice of him was a major mistake—and perhaps thought I was, too. The honeymoon was clearly over. Having been an administrator for three decades, I understood that resistance was part of the job. But this felt different. This felt like a lack of trust—in me.

None of them were putting their jobs on the line with this hire. I was. I'd long ago acknowledged the reality that every AD faces when hiring a football coach: Our futures are inextricably tied to the person we choose. If the hire succeeds, we stay. If the hire fails, we both might need to go.

Alas, Fresno State was about to shatter such conventional thinking—but in a way I never would have expected.

Chapter 15

Like a farmer whose hay was in the barn for winter, I should have relaxed. But I didn't know how—and was afraid to learn. Some in my position might have said: *You've been running at 400-meter pace for twenty-seven years, pal. Take a breather.*

Instead, I was at the office the next morning, not having been able to sleep. It wasn't the future that kept me awake, the wondering if Tedford could right the ship. No, it was the past. And not only the memories from the rectory, but now the continual guilt I felt by having to let DeRuyter go, knowing the decision that had thrown dozens of lives into turmoil. Like the incidents with Kiesle, it didn't matter that the objective facts suggested I had nothing for which to be sorry. In my mind, I was to blame.

I wrestled with my feelings. I buried my feelings. Wrestle. Bury.

Wrestle. Bury. Subconsciously, I had come to believe the way to avoid both was to dig deeper into the job. Make more donor contacts. Send more e-mails. Raise more money. Shake more hands at alumni events. Drink more wine so I could get a little sleep or stop the panic attacks and recharge whatever juice was still left in my batteries. And repeat.

Most people drink for fun. I drank for survival. It's called "self-medi-cation." Alone in the world with a secret only I knew, I would often have a glass of wine or two to calm my nerves in the wake of an "episode." To stop the shaking, slow the pounding heart, obscure the flashbacks. It was a way of coping, a strategy for dulling the pain of sexual abuse that I couldn't face. I'm not proud of that, and I'm sure at times I had more than I should have, but what other choice did I have? It was always just me and The Secret. I couldn't spill my guts to anyone. Couldn't seek advice. Couldn't make the memories go away any other way. That said, my commitment to being the best at my job—my *compulsion* with being the best—precluded such self-medication from interfering with my job. Simply put, I drank as a means of curbing the anxiety attacks whose severity few can understand unless they've endured them. I could not see any other choice.

From the day I'd started at WSU as the football manager, I'd stuck to my commitment to be the best I could be at whatever job I had. My supervisors seemed to appreciate my commitment. I was exhausted and the bags under my eyes were growing darker, but my one-year review was stellar. Of fifteen areas of effectiveness, virtually all were marked "exceeds expectations." In a 2015 review, signed by Castro, I was told I'd done "an exemplary job" and my 2016 review scores were essentially the same. Jim has "worked tirelessly to strengthen relationships with exist-ing donors and established new relationships with donors," it said. "He also has hired a talented senior team and exemplary coaches."

In May 2016, I'd posed for pictures with Castro and our new wres-tling coach, Troy Steiner, as we relaunched that program. I was running on fumes. Not eating well. Listless. My dedication to revive Fresno State athletics, my desire to appease Castro, and my desperation to do all this while slapping back the demons of the past had me running ragged. Something needed to change. And in December 2016, something did.

ONE SATURDAY MORNING I went to get a haircut. Oddly, Danielle, now fourteen, wanted to come with me; it was a rare chance to spend time with her and I relished the opportunity. When we arrived home, the street seemed lined with far more cars than usual. Peculiar, I thought. Inside, we were greeted by Eileen, her father, my mother, my son A.J., my sister Kim, and her son Drew, who had lived with us for the past year. Was this some sort of surprise party for me? A surprise party for someone else? No on both counts.

It was an intervention. It was tough love. It was a please-sign-on-the-dotted-line contract for me to enter the Sierra Tucson treatment center in Arizona, an upscale facility that treats people for an assortment of emotional problems, including PTSD, trauma, anxiety, drugs, and alcohol, you name it.

"Jim," said Eileen. "your drinking has gotten out of control."

"We're worried about you," said my mother. "You look exhausted."

"We love you, Dad," said A.J., "but you can't go on like this."

Everyone present, when it was their turn, told me how he or she was concerned about me and my health, and wanted me to get help. Nobody, I realized, had a clue what, deep down, was really wrong with me.

"Drew and A.J. will drive you to LAX," said Eileen. "Your flight leaves this afternoon."

For a split-second, my instincts were to fight the idea. Not so much out of pride but out of habit, my self-indoctrination rationalizing that I was fine, just "really busy," just "working hard." I'd never been to a therapist. I'd kept a lid on The Secret as per my unwritten agreement with myself. I could work through this on my own.

But, suddenly, amid that room full of love, it was as if decades of putting on a smiley face melted into a pool of acceptance—the idea that maybe it was OK to be the one who needs help, and to admit it to others. That my compulsion with saving Morton from the flagpole or giving CPR to Lynn Rosenbach or racing to get Harold Taylor's nitro pills or helping during the Phil Knight-UO fallout or ending the Knight-Moos Cold War or righting the Fresno State football ship—my compulsion to save others was allowing me to avoid what, in the meantime, was killing me.

I teared up and accepted hug after hug. I signed on the dotted line to be admitted to the clinic. Later, on the plane to Arizona, I began feeling an odd sense of relief. Part of it, I think, was a sense that I wasn't alone—at last. Others were in the fight with me, even if none knew my root problem—not that I understood it as anything more than a long-ago wound that wouldn't heal. Like the football player who's suffered a cramp, it was OK to take a few plays off, stretch out the leg, and get back in the game. Because, frankly, I was tired of playing hurt.

The facility wanted a thirty-day commitment, which, I figured, would work out fine. I was already planning on taking two weeks off for winter break. The campus would all but be shut down for a couple of weeks. For the third straight year, the Bulldogs weren't playing in a bowl game; no conflict there.

As the plane descended, I was equal parts eager and petrified. Eager because I sensed this opportunity to be an unexpected gift: Time to stop, explore myself, and try to figure out what was going on inside of me. Petrified for the same reasons. Indeed, the very thing that welcomed the experience frightened me as well.

Speaking of fear, when we touched ground in Arizona, I considered calling Castro but after more than forty years of keeping this secret, I wasn't ready to divulge it in a hurried phone call in the back of an Uber. *What to do? What to do?* I exhaled, stomach churning, and called my deputy athletic director, Steve Robertello. I explained that I needed some time off; I was going to Tucson for health reasons. I wouldn't have phone, text, or e-mail access after today but told him how he could reach me in any sort of emergency.

"If you need me, you can get hold of me through Eileen," I said. "I can fly back in a few hours if need be."

I texted Tedford, who was in the process of moving to Fresno from British Columbia after recently signing his contract with us. "I understand," he wrote. "I'll come see you as soon as you get back."

I arrived at Sierra Tucson, a high-brow facility in the desert that was clearly full of people with two things in common: serious emotional problems and the money—or family and friends with money—to pay for expensive treatment. It may have looked a bit country-clubish, but nobody was here for fun and games. It was, I would find, intense, demanding, rigorous.

I found myself a tad apprehensive. You don't hide in the dark for forty-four years without worrying a bit about how bright the lights might seem when you finally flip on the switch. But as I got settled in, I found Sierra Tucson was filled with people like me, trying to figure themselves out, people who were learning from other people who might know how to do that.

I was assigned to something called the all-male "Warrior Lodge." Just hearing that name triggered conflicting signals for me. I'd been a big Golden State Warriors fan as a kid, which was good, but the guy who'd taken me to a lot of Warriors games was Kiesle, which was bad. Among the thirty men in the Warrior Lodge were a former NFL star who'd been suicidal, a CEO with acute depression and suicidal thoughts, and a rock star trying to beat drugs and alcohol.

No cell phones. No TV. No communication with the outside world. From the get-go, you were made to feel that if the setting was plush the attitude was total commitment to wellness.

The first few days were about newcomers like me getting oriented—and, for many, five harrowing days in detox. So glad I didn't have to go through that. The staff began assessing what our specific problems were and how they could best treat us. Like a car owner bringing her vehicle to the shop, Eileen, when she'd phoned to make arrangements for my stay, could explain how she thought I was badly out of alignment; she believed I was an alcoholic. But it was the mechanics—the experts—who would ultimately diagnose the core problem.

I was given a physical, blood tests, and a detailed psychological questionnaire that asked dozens of questions, one of which was, "Have you ever been abused?" I didn't hesitate to answer. I checked the "no" box.

The therapist assigned to me had a wonderful English accent and was psychology's answer to Mary Poppins. Every night the doctors and therapists would meet to compare notes regarding individual patients, to see what needed to be done for whom. As Mary—not her real name—began drilling deeper into my life, I sensed she was a bloodhound looking for clues. When she had me fill out a second questionnaire, I marked boxes such as "anxiety," "trouble sleeping," and "tiredness." However, when asked if I had any abuse in my past, I again instinctively marked "no."

It wasn't until I met with seven others in a group therapy session that my armor began to crack. We were each challenged to tell who we were and why we were there. I was a bit fearful; I had never had a therapy session in my life. But I *was* a negotiator, a broker of sorts. I'd learned the art of what to say and what not to say. I could handle this.

"My name's Jim," I said.

"Hi, Jim," everyone said, as if part of an automatic-reply line.

"My problem is anxiety and insomnia, which leads to self-medication at times. If I'm having a panic attack during the day, I'll have a glass of wine at lunch. And to sleep I'll have a couple of glasses of wine, maybe a Tylenol PM. Self-medication." For me, it had never been about getting drunk. It had been about coping. Although I was unable to completely blot out the nights in the rectory, the wine at least turned the crystal-clear memories into more diffused images, softening the hurt, and enhancing my chances of falling asleep or stilling the anxiety.

"Nothing seems to work. I don't sleep. But I work hard all day long. I'm in a high-stress job where lots of people expect big things from me so I feel a lot of pressure. And when I come home, I'm tired and already worried about not sleeping so I have a couple glasses of wine—you get the idea. The cycle repeats."

The facilitator encouraged questions from the others.

"How long has this trouble sleeping been going on?" someone asked.

"Since I was a little kid. About age seven."

From the corner of my eye I saw Mary's eyes squint just a bit. She typed something on her iPad. The session ended. I left, surprised at my vulnerability; I'd never shared that deeply with anybody, including Eileen. But Mary, obviously, sensed we were only scratching the surface of Jim Bartko.

"Jim," she said afterward, "let's meet one-on-one tomorrow morning."

"Fine," I said.

I really liked her. She seemed compassionate and genuine, not someone who needed to remind you that *she* was in control and *you* weren't. The next morning, she began by saying she was curious about my insomnia beginning at such a young age.

"Most little boys sleep like rocks," she said. "To start, tell me about your family—you have one older sister, correct?"

"Correct. Kim. Two years older. Love her. Great family. Mom sacrificed for everyone around her. Dad could be strict, but he worked hard, took me to games, coached my baseball team, stuff like that."

"And did anything happen to your life about then that might have led to this trouble sleeping?"

I shook my head. "Nope." By now, the self-protection was ingrained so deeply that the lies not only came without remorse, but without awareness. Never mind that Kiesle was staring at me every time I looked at myself in a mirror, I'd conditioned myself to believe he'd never touched me.

"So, you were a happy little boy—your questionnaire says you enjoyed sports."

"Loved sports, yeah. Always have."

"What do you love about sports?"

"I love that everybody has their part and if you play your part well the team wins. Love how sports can bring people together. Fans, donors, coaches, players. They can make us better as people. In colleges, they can make the academic side of the school better. And they're just plain fun, a great diversion, I suppose, when you're going through hard times."

"And have you been?"

"Yeah, I suppose."

"So, you were a happy little boy who enjoyed sports—and then suddenly you couldn't sleep at night."

Her sentence all but fell off a ledge. She let the silence do the talking, the probing, the convicting. I readjusted myself in my chair, suddenly feeling a tad unsettled.

"Jim, one of the keys to your getting better is having the courage to be completely honest. You understand that, right?"

My head started nodding "yes" as if I were a bobblehead doll.

"Is there something that happened when you were a little boy, something that's perhaps difficult to talk about?"

For a moment, I was back in Modesto as a fourteen-year-old when

Mom asked if Father Steve had done anything inappropriate to me. I didn't speak up. I couldn't. People I loved and cared for would get hurt if I did. I couldn't let that happen. Plus, there was a monster outside the window, lurking. *I* could get hurt. And I couldn't let that happen either.

I was caught between fear and shame.

"Jim?"

Here was a second chance, the opportunity to redeem myself.

"Can you tell me what happened?"

I bent over and placed my face in my hands. *The bedroom. The candles. The wine.*

As usual, I was all but *willing* myself to forget.

"There's no shame in honesty," said Mary. "It's honesty that unlocks the things that've been holding us back—and perhaps the things at the root of our problems."

I teared up. I began to cry. I wept uncontrollably.

She handed me a tissue. I wiped my eyes. Blew my nose. Regrouped. I reminded myself that this wasn't her first rodeo; she dealt with this all the time. And was here to help me.

"We would … sometimes … go into Oakland for … Golden State basketball games," I said. "They were the Warriors—just like our lodge name."

"'We?'"

"My buddies and I, mainly my best friend, Robbie."

"And who took you to these games? A parent or *parents* I presume."

I exhaled. Looked away.

"No, our, uh, basketball coach."

"And who was that?"

I cleared my throat. I hadn't said the man's name aloud in nearly half a century and I didn't want to say it now. Her eyes widened, her head nodding slightly in encouragement.

"Jim?"

"It was, uh, Father …"

She waited patiently for seconds that seemed like minutes. When satisfied I wasn't going to drop the second shoe, she said, "Jim, can you tell me his name? Was it a priest?"

I hesitated. Sniffed. Wiped my eyes. It wasn't too late to call an audible at the line of scrimmage; I'd been doing it all my life. Instead, I nodded at her iPad.

"Google Kiesle. Father … Steve … Kiesle."

She looked at me oddly, as if wondering where this was going.

"K-i-e-s-l-e," I spelled. "Stephen."

She tapped her iPad. Waited. Tapped. Looked more closely at her screen, her eyes widening. She showed me the Web page she was on. It was the 2010 *Oakland Tribune* article about Kiesle having been released from prison after six years, then one I'd seen at the hotel in Berkeley.

"Oh, my God," she said. "Jim, are you telling me that you were one of his … ."

I nodded yes. My face warmed. Another wave of tears crashed, a virtual tsunami. She handed me more tissues.

"I am so sorry, Jim."

Since that night in 1972 when it first happened, nobody had ever said that to me. It felt strangely comforting. Finally, someone was in my corner. I can't emphasize enough how lonely I'd been over the decades, unwilling to share my story and, thus, unable to feel any empathy from others. Now I felt utter relief.

The room went silent. She said nothing. I said nothing. But I'd said it. I'd said his name. As small a gesture as it might have seemed, it was huge for me. It was acknowledgment to myself that I hadn't just been making this up. It *happened*. He *did* that to me. And Mary's affirmation soothed my aching soul. It was like that moment after you've thrown up and you're hot and sweaty and spent, as if you thought you were going to die, but suddenly start feeling better, as if you might actually *live*.

"How old when it started, Jim?"

"Seven."

"And it lasted how long?"

"Just short of … three … years."

"And so it would happen after these games that this, uh, man took you to?"

"First, he'd take us for dinner on the way home."

"Grooming you."

"What?"

"Grooming. Earning your trust. Making you like him. Perhaps making it feel a bit like you owed him something in return for ball games and dinner."

"Yeah."

"And where would this abuse happen?"

I cleared my throat, which was getting drier by the minute. "He'd take us to the rec—. To the rectory. The church rectory."

Her brow furrowed. "That seems like an odd place to go at night, after coming back late from a game. Why there?"

I swallowed hard. "Sleepovers. We had sleepovers."

"Sleepovers at the rectory? And your parents knew about these sleepovers?"

"Yeah. They were good with it. Everyone liked Father St—. Everyone liked the guy."

"So, it's Father Steve and you and a handful of your buddies staying all night at the rectory?"

"Sometimes, but usually just Robbie and me."

"OK, just the two of you and Father Steve."

I nodded yes, looked at the door, and wanted to be somewhere else, anywhere else.

"How often?"

I'd never done the math. Now, I did so. The answer shocked even me.

"I'd say about thirty or thirty-five times."

She bent forward, eyes locked on mine.

"Jim, you've done nothing wrong. You understand that, right?"

"Yes, I understand," I said, even though I hadn't thoroughly convinced myself.

"Thank you so much for sharing your pain. That took a lot of courage. Now, remember this moment. This is the moment you turned your back on *him* and stood up for *you*. We're going to help you get better, Jim."

I mouthed a "thank you" to her. It was the first time anyone had expressed that kind of empathy to me. For the first time in memory I felt no sense of shame. I exhaled, feeling good that, finally, I'd told someone that between the years 1973 and 1975, mainly in the rectory of St. Joseph

Catholic Church in Pinole, California, Father Steve Kiesle had sexually molested me an estimated thirty to thirty-five times.

Chapter 16

After Mary huddled with the rest of the facility's team that night, they ran me through more questionnaire hoops that were specific to molestation. They fine-tuned their treatment to address the roots of my trauma. Every thirty minutes people would come in to make sure I was OK—suicide watch. They discovered I wasn't just a guy who couldn't sleep and self-medicated to overcome it. This isn't about alcoholism, I was told; this is about post-traumatic stress disorder (PTSD), a mental health condition that's triggered by someone having experienced or witnessed a terrifying event. The symptoms—flashbacks, nightmares, and severe anxiety—sounded familiar.

For emergencies, we were allowed to make an occasional phone call or send an e-mail. After careful consideration, I e-mailed President Castro and told him where I was and why. I told him about the childhood sex abuse, which was difficult but, I felt, necessary. It made me feel vulnerable, edgy, worried about where this might lead, but I respected him and trusted him. And Mary had said it was up to me regarding how, or if, I divulge the new discovery to those around me.

"You're the first one I've told so I'd appreciate it if you'd keep it quiet until I get back and decide how to handle this," I wrote.

"I had no idea you were going through this," he wrote back. "I'm sorry. Take care of yourself and we'll talk when you get back."

His empathy warmed me. It felt good to be understood. Affirmed.

But, frankly, when I had a chance to collect myself, I panicked a bit. Like: *What the hell did I just do?* Telling the story inside the rehab facility seemed safe; but suddenly my secret, like Pandora's Box, had been let loose to the world. It was freeing and frightening at the same time.

That night at the Warrior Lodge, when everyone was debriefing about their days, I came clean with the guys, too.

"How was your day, Jim?" someone asked.

"Actually, it was tough. Really tough."

"How come?"

"For the first time since I was a kid, I talked about some stuff I'd been burying, some stuff I'd never shared with anyone, ever."

I told them a short-form version of what I'd told Mary. When I finished, with my tears flowing, the place erupted into applause. Suddenly, the men were standing, pumping their fists, leaning in for handshakes and hugs. No Autzen Stadium crowd had ever moved me like this.

Later, a rock singer, bald with a tattoo on seemingly every part of his body, came to my room and gave me a happiness-and-strength necklace featuring a Buddha face. His daughter had given it to him when he was on stage at a concert.

"It's to remember your new beginning," he said. "To remember your strength. And the family we've become."

For the next two weeks, I spent countless hours talking with Mary, learning where I'd been, where I was now, and where I needed to be. She had me draw a life map, a timeline of highs and lows that pinpointed not only what I was doing but how I was *feeling* about it— complete with photos and headlines cut from magazines. I bonded more closely with the guys in the Warrior Lodge. And I grew nervous on the eve of what was called "family week." This was an opportunity for each person's family to come, check out the facilities, and be involved in intense therapy with their loved one. Eileen and my mother, Mary Jane, were coming on my behalf.

If apprehensive, I was also hopeful. This would be difficult for my mother, but I figured she'd feel empathetic to what I'd been through. And even though Eileen hadn't seemed particularly interested when I'd given her the Kiesle newspaper story, this therapy experience had been her idea. I hoped she, too, would feel my pain and help me get better—once she finally learned the truth.

In fact, I was stoked that she was coming. I'd worked my tail off at Tucson Sierra. I'd spilled my guts a number of times, listened intently to the advice I'd been given, and—despite a fear of heights—done this mini-bungie-jumping test that I hadn't thought I could do. I couldn't wait to tell Eileen how far I'd come.

When she arrived, however, she seemed decidedly chilly. She seemed unimpressed with the facility, unsympathetic toward me, and uninspired by the progress I told her I was making. It was as if she was there but *not there*. But I chalked up her aloofness to it all being perhaps overwhelming to her and hoped she would warm up as the week unfolded. Maybe I was so eager to have her support me that I exaggerated anything that didn't look like 100% buy-in. Maybe I needed to understand that whatever I was going through, it wasn't just *my* problem, but the *family's* problem. Maybe I needed to be patient with her.

Day One was low-key, nothing more than a chance for the visitors to understand what Sierra Tucson was and how the staff was trying to help their loved one. But Day Two got intense. With a handful of others in the room—some Warrior brothers and staffers—Eileen and my mother would each have a chance to say to me whatever they wanted: How I'd hurt them, for example. Later, in another session, I'd have a chance to respond, but for now the facilitators, including Mary, encouraged frank, honest, gut-level communication, though with the goal of helping and not hurting.

Before she spoke a word, you could tell this was hard for my seventy-four-year-old mother. She wasn't used to anything like this, particularly with a crowd watching. But encouraged by the facilitator that this was a safe place for the greater good of me and my relationship with the family, she began. Mom looked at me, already fighting back tears.

"I guess I'd start by saying I love you and I think you're a"—the tears began—"a great … son. You never caused your father and I any trouble to speak of.

"When we left Modesto for Spokane and you chose to stay and finish high school, it hurt me deeply. But I understood why you made that choice, even if it took some time.

"We're proud of the man you've become, proud of your family, proud of all that you've accomplished at Oregon and Cal and Fresno State. But you've paid a horrible price. You work so hard and you're worn down and you look *old*, Jimmy. You look older than you are. And we just all want you to slow down and get well again."

Mom hadn't said much to spark questions or comments from the others so now it was Eileen's turn. She was "night" to Mom's "day." Without hesitation, my wife unleashed what seemed like a lifetime of anger at me about how I never opened up to her, always pretending everything was fine; how my drinking had gotten out of control; how I could never check my job at the door; and how she and the kids paid the price for my being so busy all the time. Some of it I couldn't deny; though I didn't believe I was an alcoholic, the pattern of self-medicating with wine had gotten worse. And, as she said, I could be a closed book. But I loved my kids and had always tried to be there for them. The bitterness in her delivery rocked me.

"For our entire marriage you've hidden from me whoever it is you really are," she said. "I wonder if I even know who you are anymore."

Her wrath was palpable, and when she finished, the facilitator encouraged questions or comments. Two or three guys spoke up, saying they hadn't known me long but that they saw a different Jim Bartko than she did.

"Jimmy seems to be a caring and conscientious person," one guy said.

"Courageous," someone piped in. "He's emerged as a leader in our Warrior Lodge."

"He's not perfect; he'll admit that. But he loves you guys. That's clear. He loves his family. Always talking about you guys."

I looked at Eileen, whose expression suggested she knew a different Jim Bartko than they did—or wondered if they've been conned by me. Mary apparently noticed Eileen's resistance. She scheduled a family session for 4 PM—me, Mom, Eileen, Mary, a doctor, and a therapist. This was starting to feel like crunch time. I sensed that the talking stick was being handed to me this time, and I was right.

THAT AFTERNOON, MARY introduced the session by saying this wasn't a time for me to respond to what I'd heard earlier. She had something more important for me to do.

"Jim, I need you to tell your mother and wife what you told me earlier, about your childhood in Pinole. What happened to you."

I froze in unmitigated fear. But having been at Sierra Tucson for more than three weeks, the courage to bare my soul had grown stronger. My words came slowly, but they came.

"Starting when I was seven years old … in Pinole, California … I was … sexually abused … by Father Steve Kiesle, my basketball coach … for nearly three years … maybe three … dozen times."

Mother burst into tears as if in a courtroom and I'd just been sentenced to life in prison. Eileen crossed her arms, looking suspicious.

"Mary Jane, what would you like to say to Jim?" asked Mary.

Mom dabbed her eyes with a wadded-up tissue.

"Oh, honey, I'm so, so sorry you've had to go through this. When I heard that Father Steve had been arrested for molesting children, I asked you if one of those children had been you and you told me no. I wasn't sure you were telling the truth so I asked you again, and again you told me no. And I so wanted to believe that. But I *knew*. I knew like mothers just *know*. I'm so sorry your father and I didn't protect you from that man like we should have. So, so sorry."

"Mom," I said, "there was nothing you could have done."

She just kept sobbing. Tears slid down my face. Eileen's face stayed unchanged, as if chiseled in stone.

When the talking stopped, Mary taped the life map I'd drawn to the wall.

"Jim has drawn this life map to show you his perceptions of the highs and lows of his life," she said, "and the emotions he felt along the way. One of the first entries, between the ages of seven and eight, was the headline "Frozen moment." Beneath it I'd written "Abuse begins … scared … guilt … embarrassed."

My mother walked to the map and started taking a closer look. Eileen didn't get out of her chair. Mary, the therapist, looked at Eileen.

"Eileen, how does this make you feel? Any differently?"

Eileen's body language suggested she wanted nothing to do with this. True, sending me to this facility had been her idea. But whatever outcome she expected, I sensed this wasn't it. On one hand, I wanted to shoulder the blame, say "sorry, it's all my fault that you're having to go through this." On the other hand, I was sensing some hope for the first time since I was six.

After a few minutes of back-and-forth between her and Mary, I perceived that either she wasn't tracking about my having been abused or she was but didn't care.

"Eileen?" prompted Mary.

"If Jim won't agree to stop drinking," she ultimately said, "I'm leaving."

"Eileen, that's not going to help Jim get—"

But it was too late. Eileen was already out the door. She was headed back to Fresno.

Two days later, on the flight home to Fresno, I pondered what was going on with Eileen. Initially, I wondered if she was so convinced that I was an alcoholic that she refused to accept the deeper explanation for my struggles. On the other hand, there was no denying that, even if I wasn't an alcoholic, my numbing the pain with wine had taken its toll on our marriage. In either case, I'd probably been so focused on my own struggles that I hadn't been as sensitive to her needs as I might have been.

Sierra Tucson had run numerous tests on me and, obviously, interviewed me thoroughly enough that my deepest secret came forth. The diagnosis wasn't that I was an alcoholic, but that I was suffering from

Post-Traumatic Stress Disorder (PTSD) resulting from childhood sex-ual abuse. Desperate to cope, I'd tried to do so the only way I knew how: self-medication, mainly with night-time wine. My performance improvement plan from Sierra Tucson made no reference whatsoever to alcoholism; at the rehab center, I'd gone thirty days without a drink, and that part of the stay had not been a struggle. Sierra didn't send me home with instructions to attend Alcoholic Anonymous meetings, it sent me home with a few "starter tools," coping mechanisms to help me when the anxiety welled up. Things such as breathing exercises, mind-focus exercises, books, and an encouragement to eat better, exercised, consider yoga and establish a relationship with a local therapist.

When my plane touched down—a subdued Eileen was there to pick me up—I was not the man I'd been when I left. But neither was I sud-denly "healed." You don't undo forty-four years of guilt and shame with a month's worth of therapy. I was starting a process, one of those two-steps-forward-one-step-backward propositions. But, best of all, I was *starting*. For the first time in my life, I felt as if I had a few tools—not many, but a few—to help cope with my past.

Mary wanted me to do four things: write a letter to the "young Jimmy" to relieve him of the anxiety; write an overview of my life to this point; reconnect with Robbie, the boy who'd been abused at the rectory along with me; and decide to whom, and how, I was going to disclose what I'd been through.

I began with the latter. I gathered A.J. and Danielle to tell them the truth I'd been hiding for so long. It was early January; I'd missed Christ-mas and New Year's. A.J. was still home on winter break from Loyola-Marymount. I suggested we watch the movie *Spotlight,* which I'd heard about in Tucson. It's about a *Boston Globe* investigation into how the city's Catholic diocese was hiding the sexual abuse of children by some of its priests. When the movie ended, I turned to my children, heart pounding, throat dry; just watching the movie had been difficult because it brought back my abuse. I exhaled.

"In a different time and place," I told them, "I was like those victims."

My children were teenagers, not inclined to show lots of outward emotion to their fuddy-duddy father. And they didn't. But both gave me hugs. I sensed a smidgen of understanding and a host of confusion, Danielle experiencing more of the latter than A.J. Who could blame her? It wasn't as if I'd told the kids I'd once spray-painted the neighbor's cat when I was a kid growing up in Pinole. Instead, I'd told them I'd been sexually violated by a priest for nearly three years.

To expect them to instantly understand, pledge 100% support, and return to their regularly scheduled lives was unrealistic and unfair on my part. I remembered what Mary had told me—*one day at a time*—and carried on. I told them I knew this had to be difficult for them, and offered to answer questions they had. I think they were too blown away to ask any.

The second thing I did was send a group e-mail to my staff at Fresno State and divulge the truth to people who I'd worked with for two years but who I didn't know particularly well. The response from most touched me.

"Just wanted to send you a quick note expressing how much I admire your courage in sharing something so personal with me and the department," wrote one guy. "Please continue to take care of yourself and family, as you continue to lead the department. I am here to help and support you any way I can."

That was tremendously encouraging. Next I shared my revelations with President Castro and his six-person cabinet. Unlike in his e-mail to in Arizona when I'd first told him, he seemed quiet, reserved, unsure of how to respond and what he should do. However, Adishian-Astone, his top administrator, seemed genuinely empathetic.

"Facing that," she told me, "is brave."

Two others, when I returned to the office, gave me huge hugs. One of our marketing people took me aside.

"Look, Jimmy, I don't know if you want to go public with this …"—uh, oh, was I supposed to keep this a secret?—"… but if you do, I've got the perfect person to contact at the *Fresno Bee*. She'd be great. She'd *get it*."

"Sounds good," I said. "Thanks."

He grabbed one of his business cards and jotted the name "Carmen George" on it. I stuffed it in my shirt pocket.

ONE OF THE last things my therapist reminded me was that I got to choose how open to be with what had happened to me. As January 2017 deepened, frankly, I was enjoying the new freedom of full disclosure. I was sleeping better—not great, but better. And, I'd noticed, the slight stammer I'd had was dissipating. After a lifetime of hiding, it felt good to tell the whole truth. I'd always valued genuineness in people, but in that regard I hadn't been walking the talk myself.

What's more, for the first time, I began thinking about how silence favors the Kiesles of the world, those who prey on others and too often get away with it. How darkness hides them and light makes them scurry, like cockroaches in a pitch-black basement when someone flicks on a flashlight.

"All the perpetrator asks is that the bystander do nothing," writes Judith Herman, a highly regarded psychiatrist and trauma expert. "They appeal to the universal desire to see, hear, and speak no evil. The victim, on the contrary, asks the bystander to share the burden of pain."

With some exceptions, I sensed that was happening. That people were supporting me in this struggle. And yet it was always a two-steps-forward-one-step-backward proposition.

One night, just before I fell asleep, I realized something that, at first, was painful, then hopeful. I thought back to that day in 1978 when Mom had asked if Kiesle had made me "feel uncomfortable" in any way. That day when I'd hidden the truth. Now, I thought of how many of those scores of children who were abused by the man might never have gone through that horror had I had the courage to speak up and he'd been arrested, convicted, and put in prison.

That hurt. Oh, how that hurt. I knew the pain Kiesle had caused me. And I realized that, in a sense, I had been complicit in exposing other people to the same kind of pain because of my silence. Still, I rationalized it's better late than never. I don't know where I heard it, but it seemed the appropriate metaphor for me now: *The best time to plant a tree was a hundred years ago. The second-best time is now.*

In the morning I told Eileen a plan I had; she responded with a sense of resignation rather than support. Looking back, I should have tried to understand where she was coming from. I should have been less concerned about what I needed right now and listened to what she needed; as with the kids, this all had to be rocking her world. Alas, after four decades of hiding, now that I was suddenly "free" my enthusiasm channeled into helping others, even if, at times, I overlooked the people closest to me in the process.

I picked up my cell phone.

"Hello," I said, "could I please speak to one of your reporters, Carmen George?"

Chapter 17

The decision to go public didn't come after consultations with people at the university, with friends, and certainly not with Eileen. I didn't contemplate it for days or pray about it. Instead, after four decades of silence, I simply knew the abuse was nothing I wanted to ever again keep quiet in any way, shape, or form. To do so was to only propagate the idea that I should be ashamed of—or blamed for—something that I hadn't done but had been done to me. It was to no longer inadvertently protect the bullies who did this to children. I simply knew in my heart I could never again be silent on the subject.

If this is what I needed to do, I wasn't in a place to fully weigh how the revelation might impact others. I thought about it, yes. But, in Arizona, the dammed-up waters of my emotional reservoir had been released; now there was no holding them back. I had to go with the flow. The last thing I wanted to do was hurt those closest to me—Eileen, A.J., Danielle, and my folks. At the time, I figured the best way for me to help them was for me to get better. And part of getting better, I'd decided, was to stop hiding.

The article was the lead story on the front page of the January 14, 2017, *Fresno Bee*. My marketing colleague was right. George did a great job. She didn't make excuses for me. She didn't go out of her way to paint me in a favorable light. She simply told my story. And let me offer advice to others who had been through what I'd been through.

"Don't be ashamed," I said. "Don't hide it. Hiding it doesn't do any good, because at some point it's going to come out. Bad things can happen if you suppress your feelings, and I've felt some of those. … Holding it in doesn't do anybody any good. There's help out there."

But I was about to learn that there's also a price to pay for going public, sometimes a big price. I knew when the story appeared my life would never be the same. And that I would prove to be right. In the movie *Field of Dreams,* the little girl of the guy who built the baseball field in his Iowa cornfield (played by Kevin Costner) falls off the bleachers; the suggestion is that she might die because there's no doctor around. Suddenly, one of the ballplayers from the past, Moonlight Graham—we already know he had become a doctor in his grown-up life—hustles over from the baseball field. In this fictional fantasy, he knows that once he steps over the gravel line there's no going back to being young again, and to playing ball. But he crosses the line anyway, becomes a doctor again, and saves the little girl's life.

I knew this article meant crossing the line for me. There would be no going back to the way I was before. And I was OK with that. This was the right thing to do—not just for me but for all the other victims out there who thought they were alone. And for the monsters like Kiesle who thrive on their victims being too afraid to speak up. For my family, I considered it a lesser of two evils. I wasn't naïve. I knew there might be repercussions for them—doubt about their father, kidding from classmates who didn't understand, that sort of thing. And, in hindsight, I should have talked with them more about why I needed to do this. But to try to keep it "our little secret" seemed like only a different version of the deceit I'd perpetrated for more than four decades. Like it or not, this is who I now was.

As part of the *Bee's* package on me, the newspaper included a statement from Bishop Michael Barber of the Diocese of Oakland. He said he was "deeply sorry" for the hurt Kiesle had caused.

"While I know my predecessors and others moved as quickly as they could to remove his access to children, the pain that he inflicted on vulnerable young people is a crime and a sin," Barber wrote. "The Diocese has provided counseling and other services to all who have brought credible allegations of clergy abuse to our attention. We continue to do so."

Moved as quickly as they could to remove his access to children? Was he kidding? It took six years after Kiesle's conviction in 1978 for the Vatican to defrock him, the holdup largely because of a future pope, then-Cardinal Joseph Ratzinger. And during part of that six years, Kiesle was allowed to serve as a youth volunteer at the church where he'd abused me. But I was glad to hear Barber was deeply sorry—and that counseling was available.

Toward the end of the story, George wrote—and it was true—that I was "eager to hear from community members about how he can partner with others to help stop child abuse. He wants to speak more about the issue to promote education and awareness."

She ended the piece with this quote from me: "I love what I do. I love people and kids and family. Now I've got to come to grips with my past, but it's not going to stop me. It's not going to rule who I am."

The response was fast, furious, affirming. Among the first notes I received was one from our new football coach, Jeff Tedford, and one from Phil Knight. Jeff promised any help he could give. Phil said, "I'd heard you took a short leave. Good for you. I never would have known all of what you've gone through. I'm so sorry. You've established a great career, and there's more to come. You have a great family, a successful life. You should be immensely proud of yourself. I'm here to support you any way I can."

Those words of affirmation meant the world to me. But the feedback that touched me even deeper came from other victims who had been molested.

"I read your story about your childhood recently. This summer I had to explain to my parents why a certain member was not welcomed to my wedding. Thank you for sharing your nightmare. I hope to get the chance to shake your hand and thank you in person. Your story is a reminder that I can overcome this." It was written on the letterhead of another Mountain West Conference football program.

"I wanted to write you to let you know how much I admire your courage in speaking out about your childhood experience," wrote a conference associate athletic director. "I can't imagine the difficult times you have faced, but I know your public conversation about child abuse will help many others in this country in facing their issues. Have enjoyed getting to know you and work with you and have respected your accomplishments. My respect rises to a new level."

One letter was from an author of teen fiction books that focused on edgy topics. She thanked me for my willingness to go public with a topic that most people are afraid to share. She said that because she wanted to make her books realistic, she would often interview young people facing the trials she wrote about in her book: she spoke with pregnant and parenting teenagers, a high school senior who'd come out as a lesbian, an acquaintance-rape victim.

"But," she wrote, "I was unable to interview any boys for *Shut Up.* Maybe there was some boy, somewhere, who would have been able to talk about such an experience, but I sure couldn't find him. I think I got it right, though. Since the publication [of the story] I've had a few e-mails from boys who've had such experiences, thanking me for letting them know they're not alone."

The e-mails, text messages, spoken words, and letters kept coming, dozens of them over the next few weeks.

From a fellow victim: "Like you this also happened to me and like you I have had problems overcoming this. I really appreciate your coming forward like this as a person in your position. It has inspired me to continue with my therapy and maybe explore some group therapy."

From a Duck fan back in Oregon: "I just want you to know how very proud I am of you for lifting what I hope is a huge weight off your shoulders by getting counseling and help for all the horrible abuse you suffered as a child and have carried with you for so many years. You will be in our thoughts and prayers as you continue to heal and reach out to others. Godspeed."

From someone whose business worked closely with Fresno State's athletic department: "You have always been a great guy, a terrific client, and someone that so many of us have enjoyed working for and spending time with. Your honesty and courage to share your experience takes your awesomeness to a whole new level. I am in total awe of your bravery! What a tremendously benevolent role model you are. With much love and immense respect."

From a Fresno State fan, a male: "Be bold. The motto of Fresno State, the motto of your actions. You, sir, have exemplified the qualities of boldness and courage. Not many would make the step of admission, few the step of transparency, and fewer still a proclamation publicly. Yet by doing so you have brought healing out of darkness. Our Lord tells us that sin cannot remain in the light of the Lord. Men choose to remain in darkness, but you have chosen to shine light upon the darkness. Not only for yourself but others as well. I, too, have had a similar experience and your heartfelt transparency lifted me up. God can make brokenness into glory. May he continue to walk with you on this journey."

From a Catholic woman who worked for the NCAA: "You are the bravest man I know. Wow. I am so impressed with your honesty. I am excited for what the next steps in life are going to be for you. No one deserves more. I'm a Catholic girl and I will be saying a few 'Our Fathers' and 'Hail Marys' for you. I cannot tell you how deeply moved I was when I read your story. You are a hero. Hope you know it."

When a Fresno State University organization against sexual abuse caught wind of my story a representative invited me to speak at a Sexual Abuse Awareness event. I did so, to 300 people. The presence of one, in particular, touched me deeply: Robbie's sister, Teri. I learned that she, too, had been molested by Kiesle, now her stepfather. My sister, Kim, had been a longtime friend of Teri's, going back to their days in Pinole. After I'd shared with Kim about my abuse following the intervention in Arizona, she had gotten in touch with Teri, a Fresno State alum, who showed up to support me.

The connection between Kim and Teri led to Robbie and I getting in touch with each other after more than forty years. He had, he told me, "lost everything" following years of binge drinking, but was now sober, remarried, and working as a manager for a large California landscape company. My friendship with him would become unlike any I'd ever had—we began talking regularly—because we'd shared an experience that, however horrific, bound us together.

"We're survivors," I told him.

"Well, let's just say 'we're surviving,'" he said.

On that night I spoke at the Fresno State event on childhood sex abuse, the applause and affirmation filled my soul in a way I'd never experienced. I hadn't been so upbeat in years.

Alas, it wouldn't last long. I was about to be blindsided.

Twice.

Chapter 18

When I returned from Arizona in early 2017 after seeking treatment regarding what my therapists defined as severe trauma and PTSD, my world had been rocked for better *and* worse. As I went public with my story it marked the first time since the abuse began that I didn't feel alone. But the general public was different from my family. A stranger could empathize with me—no strings attached. But it was different for those closest to me.

Everywhere Eileen went, I was now "that guy." At the grocery store, I could hear people in line whispering, "That's the guy who went public about being abused." A.J., buffered by being off at college, probably just thought it was weird. But Danielle, at fourteen, was braving the storm amid peers who, like her, couldn't begin to understand the nuances of what I'd been through. All she knew is that nobody else had a dad going public with stuff like this. And I'm sure it embarrassed her.

In hindsight, I was processing everything with too much of a "me" filter and not enough of a "those-around-me" filter. I just wanted to get well, but in my zeal to do so, I don't think I took enough time to consider how life-altering my going public with the abuse might be for my family, particularly Danielle. Overnight, the family boat was suddenly in choppy, unchartered waters, and I probably was so intent on adjusting to this "new normal" that I hadn't noticed how unsteady and afraid the rest of the crew was.

My colleagues at work seemed to understand. And the general public, based on the response from the *Fresno Bee* article, seemed to understand.

This collective affirmation was like a sip of cold water for a parched man in the desert. To look in the mirror every day and think of yourself as a victim, a failure, *weak* because you let yourself be exploited— that eats away at you little by little. Further, to know that others might have been similarly exploited because of your silence—that rubs salt in the wound.

Looking back at my life with new perspective, I felt as if I'd been losing a little bit of my soul each day, and workplace success didn't replenish that soul. I was like a lake whose inlet stream—the success of whatever school I was working for and whatever part I played in that success— could never keep pace with an outlet stream gushing with guilt and shame. Each day, the level of the lake sunk imperceptibly lower.

Given that backdrop, when I finally mustered the courage to tell my story, the response was unlike anything I could have imagined. I felt the stain of four decades wiped clean by the new realization that maybe I wasn't the culprit in all this.

Each note, whether from someone I knew or didn't, helped restore that near-empty soul.

I began sleeping better, sometimes all night long. I started eating better and drinking less. And I started using meditation and prayer almost like doctors use radiation to reduce a bloc of cancerous cells.

Meanwhile, after the *Fresno Bee* story ran, I was interviewed by an array of media outlets wanting to do stories, from *The New York Times* to ESPN to *The Oregonian*.

Although I'd never pined for the spotlight and found myself incredulous that I was suddenly speaking out about something I'd trained myself to hide, I enjoyed sharing my story.

So that's how my world was rocked for good. But here's how my world was rocked for bad: On February 3, after the media fuss died down, I was blindsided when called into President Castro's office and handed a sealed letter of reprimand. I was criticized on two counts: overstepping my bounds in negotiating Tedford's contract and leaving the university for a month without approval.

In my mind, the timing on this was suspicious. The reprimand came less than three weeks after I went public about the abuse and more than two months after Jeff Tedford's contract had been approved, signed, and celebrated by all parties, including President Castro, who now was claiming I'd built in incentives of which he hadn't approved. I had not.

Nobody, including Adishian-Astone, had been kept in the dark about these incentives, which are common for Division I football coaches and which I'd told both of them about as I negotiated with Jeff's agent. The incentives helped compensate for Jeff's base salary being $300,000 less than his predecessor's, and were needed, I felt, to help him say yes to Fresno State. Once we reached an agreement I wrote the incentives into the contract, a copy of which both Castro and Adishian-Astone were given. If they had concerns, why hadn't they shared those concerns before we'd offered Jeff the contract, before Castro had signed his name to the contract?

Further confusing me was that, initially, Castro and Adishian-Astone had both expressed empathy toward me regarding my abuse. Debbie's "facing-that-is-brave" comment was one of the most encouraging responses I'd gotten. But after I went public the weather turned chilly with both of them.

Based on Castro's reprimand, Robertello's report to the president suggested I'd basically gone AWOL with no regard for the athletic department or the university. I had not. True, I should have communicated directly to Castro. But here's what started to trouble me about that situation: as an associate AD at Fresno State and the interim athletic director

I had replaced, Robertello would potentially have the most to gain if I were suddenly out of the picture. The AD job, after all, would be open. Robertello had been in the Fresno State department since 2012 and, as the interim AD before I arrived, might have thought he would get the job I got instead.

Did Robertello skew my message? Only he knows that. But either something got lost in translation between him and Castro about my taking a mental-health break mostly during the holidays or a president who had given me stellar reviews soured on me overnight—coincidentally, shortly after I went public regarding the abuse.

What I'll own is that it was a bad choice to phone Robertello instead of Castro amid my whirlwind of emotions en route to Arizona. What I won't own is any hint that I turned my back on—or was negligent regarding—an institution that I'd grown to love and was doing my all to improve. This was not a case of Jim Bartko, without saying a word to anyone, jetting to Cancun for fun in the sun on the university's nickel. This was a man who, in the process of helping get Fresno State back on track, made a potential do-or-die trip, at his family's insistence, to restore his mental health.

Along with our dedicated coaches, student-athletes, and donors, nobody had put in more blood, sweat, and tears into breathing life back into our programs than I had in the two years I'd been at Fresno State.

Beyond the charges themselves, what seemed odd about the written reprimand was how it contradicted my performance reviews. I was blindsided only about four months after my straight-A review in which I'd been lauded by the president for my work and been praised for having "worked tirelessly to strengthen relationships with existing donors and establishing new relationships with new donors. He has also hired a talented senior team and exemplary coaches."

Given all this, when I was given the reprimand, I was numb with disbelief. Hurt. Confused. Fearful. What, I wondered, was going on here? What had changed to trigger this abrupt about-face? The only thing that came to mind, of course, was that I had gone public with the revelation that I was a child-sex-abuse survivor.

Is it possible that those same administrators saw this as an embarrassment to Fresno State, particularly because I was head of a department steeped in machismo? Was I no longer a worthy "face" for the department? If they were embarrassed, why? And if they truly believed that my discovery and decision to go public with it was adversely affecting my job performance, why not discus campus resources that might help me? Instead, I was told that I could either take a sixty-day leave to "get my act together" or face further reprimands and disciplinary action. I was given three days to choose. Unable to decide on a course of action, I chose to pass on the offer, explore more thoroughly my best options, and, on my own vacation time, seek thirty days of treatment at Passages of Malibu in the summer.

Finally, if the university didn't suddenly turn against me because I'd gone public, why would they choose this time to unleash what, beneath the veneer of the incidents at hand, seemed chillingly like a personal attack? Then I remembered the words from a high-level administrator who'd left the university—long before I'd left for Arizona—suggesting I not get too comfortable, that he'd been forced out and I might be, too.

I rationalized that couldn't be the case. I'd gone through a tough "fire" (DeRuyter) and made a potentially great hire (Tedford). My reviews said I was doing great work. Boosters and students and newspaper columnists were telling me I was a breath of fresh air, getting out in the community and meeting people, looking people in the eye. Being real with people.

Why worry?

EILEEN RECOMMENDED WE see a marriage counselor. I agreed. It was long overdue. In my zeal to do my job well, I'd put the marriage on autopilot. In my zeal to deal with the PTSD, I'd sometimes let the self-medication get the best of me. I was eager to recalibrate with Eileen now that I'd faced my past.

In early February 2017 we sat down with a female therapist who let Eileen explain first what she thought was the matter. Not surprisingly, her answer was *me*. Not that I was a perfect husband. Not that I didn't have much to improve on. But if we're all evolving as individuals, she didn't seem to be cutting me much slack; in her fifteen-minute talk, for example, she never mentioned the abuse. Not that I considered it an excuse, but it was an elephant in the room that other therapists had told me we had to face.

Next it was my turn. I didn't open fire at Eileen. However, I did mention my abuse. How could I *not*? I didn't believe I had the right, as a husband, to use the abuse as a Get-Out-of-Jail- Free card, to excuse myself for not being a better husband.

Undoubtedly, I could have been a better mate to Eileen. But if Sierra Tucson taught me anything, it was the value of opening up, which I was committed to doing more of with Eileen. I knew I had work to do to become a more engaged husband, and I looked forward to making it happen.

"It's been a tough five weeks," I said. "In fact, it's been a tough last forty-four years."

"And why is that?" the counselor asked.

"I just got back from a treatment facility where, for the first time, I talked about having been sexually molested as a kid," I said. "Over nearly three years' time."

Her eyes widened.

"Wait a minute," she said. "Timeout. You were abused as a child for three years and had told nobody until just recently?"

"Correct."

She shook her head sideways as if in disbelief. "Well, then, my apologies but this session is over."

"What?" said Eileen.

"We don't need to be mixing marriage counseling when Jim has something this significant he needs to deal with first. He needs at least six months to get healthy again, then you two come back and see me."

This, other therapists later told me, might not have the best way to address the two problems; it might have been better, they suggested, to deal with both at once since my abuse obviously impacted the marriage. But what seemed less significant to me than this therapist's divide-and-conquer approach was Eileen's response to it.

"And just what am I supposed to do in the meantime?" she asked.

"You should support Jim."

Eileen rose to her feet. "I can't do that," she said. And walked out of the room.

IF THE WRITTEN reprimand was puzzling, so was President Castro's decision to start having Adishian-Astone attend what had been our one-on-one meetings. Suddenly, what had been routine president/athletic director informational exchanges came with an ominous tone to them. Adishian-Astone and I were equals in the pecking order. So why did it suddenly feel as if she and the president were suddenly running a two-on-one fast break—and I was the lone defender?

Meanwhile, in my challenge to deal with the PTSD I'd finally faced, I felt equally alone. As good as Sierra Tucson had been for me, the treatment center had exposed my problem but hadn't given me much in the way of tools to deal with that problem. You don't fix four decades of shame and guilt and regret by simply exposing the roots of the problem. I needed more therapy—and I needed Fresno State to offer compassion, support, understanding. Alas, that wasn't happening.

In retrospect, I should have connected with a therapist in Fresno to have immediate ongoing professional support for adjusting to this new chapter in my life.

February became March. I was feeling good about the momentum we'd developed in the athletic department. Spring football had started. Tedford's arrival was already helping with fundraising. As per the president's request, I'd dutifully worked to get the men's wrestling and women's water polo programs up and running. Our athletes' GPAs were on the rise.

Then I got a second out-of-the-blue reprimand from the president. In early March, Castro told me he was starting to lose faith in me, though I never quite understood what, exactly, I'd done, or not done, to trigger this sudden loss of faith in me. His charges were vague accusations; in fact, I always got the sense that his heart wasn't in to these reprimands, that he secretly believed in me but was doing the bidding of someone else.

I was, he said, "unfocused." Things were "dropping through the cracks." I came home that night incredulous. At Fresno State, my nighttime anxiety, insomnia, and self-medication had manifested itself much as it had at Oregon and Cal: the workplace didn't pay the price, my wife and children did. That, Eileen would say, is the problem: *you give so much at work that there's nothing left for the rest of us.* I couldn't argue with that. My time of therapy in Arizona had not only eased my sense of guilt regarding the abuse and my not reporting the abuse but awakened me to the stuff at home I needed to "own." But in three decades of athletic administration I'd never been accused of letting anything slide or of ever being unfocused. What I heard more than anything from my colleagues was: "Jimmy, get your sorry ass home, pal. We can handle this. You've been here twelve hours."

The words of reprimand from Castro and Adishian-Astone settled in my stomach like battery acid. I didn't even know where to begin to defend myself. I didn't try. As I walked out of Castro's office, it seemed that, for whatever reason, I'd become the proverbial Dead Man Walking.

On March 23, 2017, Castro and Adishian-Astone called me in again. This time the subject of the reprimand was drinking alcohol while on official business—I'd been seen having a glass of wine at an Applebee's on my lunch hour while writing thank-you cards for the notes of encouragement I'd been getting. I was told "there should be very few times" I should be consuming alcohol while on university business. Beyond the drinking, I was reprimanded for inaccurate, incomplete, and late expense reimbursement requests.

Amid this puzzling finger-wagging from the president's office, a "what's-wrong-with-this-picture" scenario started taking shape. Everywhere else I looked, people were helping me—or *had* helped me. My family had cared enough about me to force me to get therapy. Friends such as Tedford and Knight offered to help in any way they could. Some of my new friends from Warrior Lodge were regularly encouraging me with e-mails. Complete strangers, after seeing my story in the media, were sending me notes of encouragement.

But my sense was that the people I reported to at Fresno State were doing just the opposite: turning their backs on me. In April, Adishian-Astone met me at a Starbucks with an obvious agenda: to inform me that essentially everyone I'd hired—fundraisers, marketing specialists, architects for the stadium remodel—were, as she termed it, "incompetent."

Then why, I wondered, were we seeing marked progress in all such areas? Why were ticket sales up? And why had President Castro, in my review, written that I'd "hired a talented senior team and exemplary coaches?" I tried pointing out such things to Adishian-Astone, but she didn't seem particularly interested, nor was I necessarily adept at standing up for myself at this point. Yes, I'd gone public with the abuse—I was standing up for survivors everywhere—but I was less inclined to defend myself.

If I was clouded about was happening before, now I was only further confused. Like most universities, Fresno State enthusiastically ran a wellness program for its employees. To read the handouts that you'd see on campus billboards, you sensed the university desired to come alongside any employee or student who was struggling and do what they could to get him or her through the rough spots. The university would go out of its way to be a safe place for the people who were part of it—and rightfully so. But that help wasn't offered to me.

True, early on, right after I'd revealed my abuse, a handful of administrators—Adishian-Astone in particular—showed empathy and offered encouragement. But once the *Fresno Bee* story hit it was as if I was contagious. After that, only a few of Fresno State's upper-echelon administrators showed me anything, on an institutional level, that spoke of grace, empathy, or encouragement. Something that said: *We're family. You're part of the family, Jimmy. How can we help?*

IN JULY, WITH plenty of advance warning for President Castro and my staff, I left for the Passages Clinic in Malibu, California, to do follow-up on how to find ways to cope with the PTSD. In Arizona, the crux of my work was simply my admitting what had happened; now I needed tools to learn how to cope with it. For athletic departments, mid-summer is the calm before the storm. From August through May I worked a lot of sixty-to-seventy-hour weeks. I was looking forward to learning more tools about dealing with PTSD and getting back in time for fall football practice to begin. I was eager to see what Tedford was going to do as our new football coach. Eager to see if, as I expected, Jeff would get us winning again and our crowds would start growing again.

Alas, an emotional grenade blew up the Malibu experience.

"Excuse me," said a courier soon after I arrived at my hotel, "are you James Bartko?"

"I am."

"You've been served."

And he handed me what I soon realized were divorce papers. In seeking to terminate our marriage, Eileen cited "irreconcilable differences." Eileen requested an emergency order to gain custody of Danielle. (By this time, A.J., at twenty-one, was no longer a minor.) In pressing for custody of Danielle, Eileen said I was "an alcoholic" and had "a history of drunk driving with me and/or my daughter in his vehicle."

"Jim's unwillingness to admit that he has a problem with alcohol places our daughter at significant risk of emotional harm," she wrote in her declaration.

FROM MY PERSPECTIVE, Eileen was missing a deeper truth: that I was willingly admitting, for the first time in more than forty years, that I had problems—but, no, alcohol wasn't the primary one. The wine drinking was a symptom of a much deeper problem that I was finally facing, a way to mask a hurt that, until now, I had no other way to deal with. In an attempt to do so, I was in the process of spending close to $200,000, between Tucson and Malibu. That didn't seem like an "unwillingness-to-admit" stance to me. Thanks to the intervention, I'd been able to pinpoint my problems. And if no professionals were treating me for alcoholism, I was nevertheless happy to own the self-medication that, even if I thought was helping me cope, I'd learned was actually working against me.

Eileen, however, had written a narrative that ignored my PTSD. Why, I'm not sure, but I've wondered if my getting slapped with the designation of "alcoholic" would officially confirm me as The Bad Guy. In her eyes, the sexual abuse may have only muddied the waters of that narrative. At any rate, when the intervention at Sierra Tucson focused on the abuse and not alcoholism, her refusal to accept my deeper problem—and partner with me in dealing with it—cut to the bone.

Don't get me wrong. I needed to take ownership for the part I played in the demise of the marriage, among it my turning to wine instead of more helpful tools in dealing with my abuse; letting work nudge aside time and attention she and the family deserved; and not being more open to her about what I was going through. But when she filed for divorce, I felt as if she'd ignored the Jim Bartko with, admittedly, plenty of baggage while creating a facsimile that worked in her favor. I'm not sure she believed she added any weight to whatever crushed our marriage. In my experience, empathy was never her strong suit. And, unfortunately for us both, she had married a man who needed some.

At any rate, the marriage was over. After twenty-three years, I was sorry I hadn't been a better husband to Eileen. But I wasn't sorry we married. Among other things, we raised two amazing children. I will forever be indebted to Eileen for that and for forcing the issue when she saw me flying too close to the ground. Without having gone to Sierra Tucson, I would probably still be harboring a secret that was eating at me—and slipping lower into the quicksand I barely escaped. Instead, that experience became the pivot upon which my life took its greatest turn for good.

After our split, I realized a sad irony: the woman who'd once again walked out on me—this time for good—was the same woman who'd set in motion what saved my life.

Chapter 19

A "whisper campaign," the dictionary says, is "a method of persuasion in which damaging rumors or innuendo are spread about the target, while the source of the rumors seeks to avoid being detected while spreading them."

In the fall of 2017, three significant things happened. First, true or not, I perceived that I'd become the target of a whisper campaign on campus. Second, Fresno State, with Jeff Tedford in charge, started winning lots of football games. And, third, fans started flocking to games; by season's end, attendance would be up an incredible 20.1%, the seventh-highest increase among Football Bowl Subdivision (FBS) teams.

By now, Eileen and I were legally separated, though still living together, the house divided in half by an invisible demarcation line. On campus, those in power said all the right things—"Sorry to hear the news, Jim"—but, I suspected that, behind my back, some used the divorce as more kindling for the rumor fire. Within weeks, I wasn't Jim Bartko, the athletic director spearheading the fight to return Fresno State football to greatness. I was Jim Bartko, who was suddenly incompetent at work and couldn't keep his marriage together.

Sometimes the truth can be complex; for a person who's never been sexually abused, it's not easy to understand what it's like to endure the aftershocks of that every day for more than 14,000-plus days. It's not easy to understand the tangled web of guilt and shame manifesting itself in PTSD. It's not easy to take a risk and do what hardly anyone connected with Fresno State was willing to do: say, "Jim, I have no idea what you must be going through. But I'd like to understand. Can you help me so I can lend my support to you in helping you get better?"

It's far easier to just assume the gossip must be true; the guy's incompetent.

Once the fire gets going, rumors take on lives of their own; tell a lie enough times, they say, and people will come to believe it. Truth is, alcohol is served at all sorts of university events; goodness, when I returned from the clinic in Arizona the president hosted a retreat for top administrators—*at a local winery.* It was common for administrators to partake—and, when they did, I don't recall other school administrators being slapped with the "drinking problem" label. And when boosters had partnered with the university to throw me a surprise birthday party four months after I'd arrived, they'd encouraged each person coming to bring me a bottle of wine; would they have done that if they truly believed I had a drinking problem?

But suddenly reports swirled of Jim Bartko over-imbibing here and there, fed to the powers that be—and sensationalized—by people who I believe had axes to grind.

Rumors are mostly projections of the individuals who started them, the people who quietly work their power plays. What gets lost in the process is any semblance of truth. The result? I was toast. How did I know? Eileen told me. She knew of the letters of reprimand before I did. She told numerous people in Fresno and Eugene that I was going to get fired. How she knew, I don't know.

All I know is that it stung. I needed support, understanding, and validation. Eileen, for her own reasons, seemed more worried about her financial future. I get it, our lives were unraveling. My disclosure set in motion a series of events that I couldn't control. But if I was struggling, I was also hopeful. In hindsight, I realize Eileen was hurting, too. But, obviously, she'd given up hope.

One night, lying in bed alone in a house I still shared with the woman who no longer wanted me, I felt as if I was not there, in Fresno. Instead, I was on Alcatraz, imprisoned. Alone. Misunderstood. With no possibility of boats arriving to get me safely to shore. Stranded in the middle of icy waters.

At home, I heard Eileen puttering here, shuffling there, but the silence between us was deafening. At work, I directed a staff in an atmosphere that, to me, seemed rife with suspicion. I knew hundreds of people but few particularly well—and the ones I did consider close friends were far away, busy, and had more important things to do than deal with my problems.

Convict Lake. You need to go to Convict Lake.

My mind took me back to a therapy session I'd had in Malibu. By then, the "find-your-happy-place" theme had become a staple on humorous greeting cards, but I'd found it to be serious—and good— therapy. When you're desperately looking for reason to go on, a happy place beats the hell out of Alcatraz.

"Jim, would you like to take a trip with me?" the therapist had said to me in a therapy session back in the summer of 2017.

"Sure, I'm game."

She had me lean back in the soft chair, eyes closed.

"Relax. Breathe deep. OK, you ready? Hold on tight."

I exhaled deep and felt totally at ease.

"We're going to a place you know well, the rectory in Pinole."

My gut lurched, heart pounded, body tensed.

"Do you see it?"

I didn't want to see it, hear of it, think about it ever again. Was this therapy or emotional water torture?

"Yes," I said with a sense of resignation. "I see it."

"Do you see the door to the bedroom?"

Really?

"Jim, what do you see? Describe it to me."

She might as well be taking me to the top of the TransAmerica building, blindfolding me, and asking me to take one step forward.

"A bed. I see a bed."

"And who's in the bed?"

"There are three of us in it. Robbie's on the left, next to the wall. Father Steve is in the middle. I'm on the right, closest to the door, curled up in a ball, back to Father Steve. Crying. Quietly crying."

"Jim," she said, her voice like butter, "would you like to get Jimmy and take him away from this place?"

"Yes, let's get Jimmy."

"And where would you like to take him? Where's a happy place for you, a place you have only good memories?"

"That's easy, Convict Lake, near Mammoth Lakes, not far from Yosemite."

"And what are you doing there?"

"In a boat with my dad and uncle. Trout fishing."

"OK, Jimmy's in the boat. And what else is going on?"

"On shore, in front of the cabin we're staying at, Mom has steaks on the grill. It's late afternoon. You can smell the smoke from the grill hanging over the water."

"Sounds wonderful," she said. "So, Jimmy, would you want Robbie to join you guys for dinner? Do you want to go get him out of the rectory?"

"Yes," I said, "let's go get Robbie."

And, as I lay in bed in Fresno, that's where I'd gone, to Convict Lake. There we all were—Robbie, Dad, Mom, Uncle Dan, and me—sitting beneath the pines on the shores of Convict Lake, a mile high in the Sierra Nevada, the granite mountains rising beyond, the outside sink cradling a limit of rainbow and brown trout, the scene wrapped in a bow of perfection and peace that lulled me, at last, to sleep.

"Jim," said President Castro, "this is not going to be an enjoyable meeting for you."

At his desk, with Adishian-Astone—as always—to his side, President Castro tried to look me in the eye without really looking me in the eye.

"We think it's time to part ways."

Blood rushed to my head. It was November 6, 2017. Two days before, Fresno State had beaten BYU to clinch its first bowl bid in the last three years. I'd expected that our pre-meeting small talk would be about this long-awaited milestone. Now this.

"We've given you chances to improve your job performance and it isn't happening. We can either fire you 'for cause' or you can resign with a minimal severance."

I didn't know quite how to respond. In more than two decades of working for athletic departments of four Division I universities, I'd never even had a negative review. Not one. Now, I was being forced to resign? Had I somehow changed?

Well, yes, in one sense I had. Eleven months before, my Sierra Tucson experience had freed me, in some ways, from forty-four years of shame and guilt. For the first time in my life I could look in the mirror and not be back in the St. Joseph rectory. I was sleeping more, self-medicating less, and learning how to better cope with the PTSD from the abuse.

Meanwhile, the football program was on the rise. Ticket sales were up. Donations were up. Wins were up. Goodness, this was the first Monday morning in three years in which our fans had awoken knowing we were headed to a bowl game; if anything, this moment should have been one of celebrating our hard work and progress. Tedford, in his first year, was putting together a season that would exceed the expectations of even our most skeptical board members. With my life suddenly infused with all this positive energy, why would this be the one time when, according to the "resign-or-else" document on the table in front of me, I would fail at my job?

I looked at the papers. The command was to sign it or trust my reputation to the very people who were forcing me out. Wasn't that the unspoken threat? Whatever the power bloc had documented as their "for cause" argument would "accidentally" get leaked to the *Fresno Bee*, a laundry list of transgressions carefully constructed to make the guy who, a year ago was given a gold-medal review, look incompetent. And I'd be powerless to defend myself.

I'd spent most of my life being defined by a man who unfairly lorded his power over me. Now, in this Fresno State office, I felt like others were unfairly lording their power over me. My reputation, if I didn't sign, would not be defined by insight from objective sources beyond the whisperers: the boosters who told me I was the first AD in a long time who got out of his office and made donors feel as if they were truly part of the Bulldog family; the reviews that lauded my performance; the hope for a turnaround that major donors told me they were starting to feel. No, these things would stay hidden in the shadows. If I didn't sign, what would make the *Bee* would be the carefully edited appraisal of me by a handful of people with an agenda, people who'd already come up with an answer for their mathematical equation—*Fresno State minus Bartko*—and, in the sealed envelope, had undoubtedly manipulated the numbers to add up to their desired result. Since I'd gone public with the abuse—and for reasons I didn't understand—some administrators had quietly declared war on me. And, as they say, the first casualty of war is truth.

"May I read it?" I asked.

"No," said Castro.

"May I speak to my attorney?"

"No."

I felt like I was back in my rental car on the Bay Bridge, wanting to stop but being forced forward by the vehicles behind, everyone wanting to get somewhere and willing to all but bump me off the bridge to do so.

I asked if I could call Eileen; the divorce was not final, and this involved her. I was told I had five minutes. I couldn't reach her. I needed more time.

"Time's up," said Adishian-Astone—again, an administrator on the same level as me. "You have to make your decision. *Now.*"

I was dumbfounded. I felt trapped, as if I had a gun to my back—and the only way out was to give in. It had been decades since those nights in the rectory, but something about this situation chilled me just the same. Different place. Different time. Different circumstances. But the same power imbalance: *I can make you do whatever I want, and nobody will ever know.*

And what was my only choice? Heart pounding, body sweating, mind racing at the insaneness of this setup, I signed—for the same reason innocent people sometimes confess to crimes. Because with the pressure on, with the clock ticking, with the inevitability of the results so apparent, what consumes your mind isn't long-term justice and certainly isn't whatever chump-change severance they would throw in to placate me, but freedom. You just want out. Now. Out of this room. Out of this situation. Out of this trap that had been seemingly planned for the benefit not of Fresno State University and certainly not for me, but for the architects of the ouster.

Castro quickly produced a second document titled "Settlement Agreement and Release" that included a waiver "of any right (Bartko) may have under law or regulation to seek reconsideration or to revoke his resignation."

Enough. I waved the white flag. I gave up. I signed, took my envelope—the severance was for just over $73,000—and started to leave.

"You'll need to clean out your office," I was told by the same president who, three years before, at the news conference announcing my hire, had said, "I am delighted that Jim Bartko is returning home to the Valley to join the Bulldog family. He has the right skills, a long track record of significant accomplishments, and he enjoys working with people."

I ignored the command and left. I no longer worked for Fresno State University.

That night the story hit the TV news, online newspapers, Twitter, you name it. The next morning someone was pounding on our door. It was a university official. He'd come for my courtesy vehicle and its keys. It was 6:30 AM

IF THAT WAS bizarre, so was a column in the *Bee* the same day that not only commented on my firing, but mentioned the divorce, complete with quotes from Eileen taken from her divorce filings. The headline said: "Why did Fresno State AD Jim Bartko leave? Divorce papers say he's battling alcoholism."

It was an interesting time juxtaposition, to say the least. Eileen had filed for divorce in July; the columnist had four months to pick up on the news—it was no secret—and report it. Instead, the divorce revelation was neatly packaged with the firing, giving the anti-Bartko brigade a powerful one-two punch—as if to suggest justice had been served.

To his credit, the columnist did point out I had never been arrested for drinking and driving, and, in fact, had no arrests, period. But he failed to mention that the divorce-court judge had enough faith in me to award Eileen and I equal access to our children—not something a judge would do if believing, as Eileen said in her divorce suit, that I "had a problem with alcohol" that placed "our daughter at significant risk of emotional harm."

Had the columnist coincidentally caught wind of the divorce just as I was fired or had someone from Fresno State, or Eileen, gone to the *Bee* at that opportune time to bolster their anti-Bartko case—or add salt to my wound? Did anyone check with Sierra Tucson about Eileen's allegations that I was an alcoholic?

I'd spent a lifetime keeping a secret about a betrayal. Ironically, now that I'd finally had the courage to reveal that secret, I was feeling even more betrayals. One of the best lessons I'd learned in Arizona—wonderfully expressed at the end of *Good Will Hunting*—was that it wasn't my fault that I'd been sexually abused. But now, in my marriage and in my job, what I was sensing took me back to the dark years of secrecy: it *was* my fault. I was left in a fog of confusion, trying to get some sort of foothold on four decades of betrayal and now sensing betrayal anew.

Wikipedia only fanned the flames of the whisper campaign, amplifying the same lies. It said—and still says—I "abruptly resigned as athletics [sic] director on November 6, 2017 due to struggles with alcoholism and a domestic separation." Patently false. First, I was forced to resign. Second, none of the doctors or therapists I'd seen in treatment centers has ever labeled me as an alcoholic. And, third, my leaving Fresno State had nothing to do with my marital status whatsoever.

History, it's been said, is written by the winners, by the people in power. I'm not a man without faults; like most people, I'm sure I turned in expense-account forms late on occasion. I'm sure I've made other mistakes, too. But Fresno State's narrative suggested that the same athletic director the university had sought, hired, and subsequently praised for his great work had suddenly turned incompetent. That someone who had never had a problem communicating to a university president what's in a football coach's contract suddenly did. Had never had a problem mixing social drinking with his job but suddenly did. Had never had a problem with allowing things to "slip through the cracks" but suddenly did.

All, coincidentally, right after that athletic director went public with the news that he'd been sexually molested as a child and finally had found the courage to speak out about it—with the intent of perhaps preventing some child somewhere from enduring similar horrors.

I was right about crossing that *Field of Dreams* line and never being able to come back. I was being told, *you can't play in our game anymore.* The trip to the get-well facility in Arizona became the perfect catalyst for a whisper campaign suggesting that I was damaged goods. A liability. Careening out of control. The divorce poured more gas on the fire, Eileen's statements in the *Bee* only further dirtying a reputation that I had no chance to defend.

Had other people been in control at Fresno State, the narrative might have been written very differently. The school might have reached out to me instead of turning its back on me. Given that the school's focus was ostensibly education, here was a teachable moment that might have showcased, on my part, the courage to seek help rather than keep suffering and, on the school's part, the grace to cut employees on the mend some slack. Win-win. Instead, Fresno State's top administrators spun it just the opposite: I was a broken man who had to be gotten rid of. Lose-lose.

A week after I resigned under pressure, I released a statement to the *Bee* that said, in part:

> These last few days, while gut wrenching in so many
> respects, have restored my belief that Fresno is full of
> solid, decent people who are unconditional in their love

of others and their embrace of what's right.

To those of you who have reached out—many fans, donors, friends, non-fans, neighbors, and acquaintances—I am so grateful and humbled. My call-outs to people of extreme character and kindness in the Valley would take many pages. I so appreciate not just your support of me, but especially your support of Fresno State Athletics and the progress we have made to make Fresno an even better place without fear that the bar might be too high.

Fresno deserves to set the highest bar in every part of our community to prove how worthy this place and its people are of greatness … . We have set in motion what it takes to raise [the] bar, and the team at Athletics I'm so regrettably leaving behind has the talent to rise above the challenges in setting and maintaining that bar. That begins with having courage on many fronts.

I have such a deep heartfelt desire for this Athletics program and for this community to succeed. That is why my departure from Fresno State hurts so much.

My journey will continue. My story will be told. Between the lines that you read in the newspaper, this is true: I am Jim Bartko, not a perfect man, who loves the mission of Fresno State, loves his family, knows what Athletics can do beyond the scores, and is willing to live in the truth come what may.

Thank you friends, and Go Dogs.

Jim

When the dust had settled, I called two close friends, former Cal quarterback J Torchio, and Renee Baumgartner, the Santa Clara director of athletics and a former colleague at Oregon.

"I'm so sorry, Jimmy," she said. "You deserved better."

The two knew each other and invited me to the Bay Area to commiserate. We were having breakfast in a Lafayette restaurant when I received a text from Eileen. She said the movers were coming and the house wouldn't have any furniture when I got back. Also, she'd taken our dog because, as her text said, she was the one who walked him so deserved him.

I sat there like a man without a country. No wife. No job. No dog. The only thing I had left was my integrity. My honor. My sense that despite my reputation having been reshaped to fit the needs of a woman who was divorcing me and a few Fresno State administrators who seemed to be abandoning me, I had, amid the second-most tumultuous time of my life, managed to save the one thing that others seemed so eager to snuff: *me*—or whatever was left.

And friends. I had my friends. In the silence of an evening alone, I could almost hear the cheers from the guys in the Warrior Lodge after I'd told them my story. Robbie was always there, a voice on the other end of the phone who understood like no others. And I felt grateful for folks such as Phil Knight and Jeff Tedford, who'd offered to help in any way they could.

Near year's end, when I returned for a second time to the Passages health care clinic in Malibu to learn more tools for recovery, friends back in Eugene passed the hat for me. They sent me a check for $90,000 to cover expenses. Included was a letter saying that this was only a token of how highly they valued their friendship with me. I was floored and flattered. I cried.

"Can I pay it back?" I asked the person in charge of the campaign.

"No, just pay it forward for someone else who needs help."

Amid the stench of betrayal, it was, for me, the sweet smell of something the world desperately needs more of—compassion.

Chapter 20

In the fall of 2018, Jeff Tedford led Fresno State's football team to a 12-win season, the best in school history. The Bulldogs, in only Jeff's second year, trounced the Pac-12's UCLA 34-14 in the Rose Bowl stadium, won the Mountain West Conference championship with a victory over Boise State on the Broncos' snow-swept blue turf, and beat Arizona State in the Las Vegas Bowl.

"Jeff Tedford," wrote the sports website SBNation, "was the best hire of 2016," pointing out that Fresno State was 4-20 in the two years before I hired him and 22-6 after.

My e-mail box and Twitter account were flooded with messages from Fresno State fans thanking me for hiring the guy.

"You created this," wrote another with three thumbs-up emojis. "Thank you."

"Unfortunately, no one will give you credit for the success everyone is enjoying from football," said another. "You hired Tedford, but nobody talks about that. Thank you!"

By far the most common question that boosters, friends, and others asked after my dismissal was: *Why?* I still wonder myself. Did Adishian-Astone—my equal on the university's hierarchy—want me out as part of an aggressive quest for more power? It was no secret she wanted authority over the athletic department's budgets and projects, a shift I didn't think was in the best interest of the university. Did Robertello believe he could leverage my trip to Arizona and the rumors of alcoholism as a way to get me out—and himself in—as athletic director? Only they knew.

Not surprisingly, it was bittersweet, frankly, seeing the Las Vegas Bowl awards ceremony on TV. I was so proud of Tedford and our football program for doing what so few believed could be done, and felt envious watching President Castro and Adishian-Astone up on that stage, basking in the glory, smiling broadly regarding a coach who Castro was slow to buy into and who Adishian-Astone resisted hiring.

Soon after I left Fresno State, Adishian-Astone was, as I expected, named the university's permanent chief financial officer and human resources director. Among her new areas of responsibility: authority to oversee athletics budgets and projects. I wasn't surprised.

Robertello was named interim athletic director. The new world order was emerging just as I thought, though I was later surprised when Robertello didn't get the permanent position. Instead, in June 2018 Fresno State hired Terry Tumey, a former NFL executive who'd been AD at University of California-Davis. What I knew of Tumey suggested he was a first-class hire and I wished for him and Fresno State nothing but success, to build on whatever foundation I had helped rebuild. Robertello was reassigned to a position beneath Adishian-Astone called "Special Assistant to the Vice President for Student Affairs and Enrollment Management," and separated from the university in June 2019.

As Tedford was basking in his well-deserved glory, I had moved back to Eugene, at first feeling like a stranger in a strange place. I'd been gone nearly three years. When Eileen, without even consulting me, had taken our dog, it had wounded me deeply. So, one of the first things I did was get a new dog, Stella, an English Golden Retriever, named by Danielle. At first, I was as lost as I'd ever been. Marriage gone. Job gone. Reputation gone. And though dealing better with my boyhood wounds, still aware that the trauma could be tamed, but never completely muzzled. Now, one rainy night, I was as low as I'd been in a long time.

I had never seriously considered taking my life, but on this night, wrestling to get to sleep, I did wonder: *can I go on?* Not long ago I'd been married, the head of a Division I athletic program, making good money, and living in a four-bedroom house with a pool. Now I was living alone in an apartment over a pizza place. No job. No wife. No sense that I was making any sort of difference in the world. And why? Because I'd stepped over the first base line on that mythical field of dreams. Because I'd dared to go public as a means of helping put an end to the same abuse that had tarnished my life.

Had it been worth it? At times, I'd wondered, like on nights like this when I'd wake up and the silence would mock me, as if to say: *You never should have told. Silence keeps the waters smooth. Talking makes waves.*

I got up to go the bathroom, lay back down on the bed. Stella jumped up on the bed and laid down beside me. Her eyes were filled with what appeared to be understanding, as if she were saying: *I got you. You're gonna be OK, Jimmy. You're gonna be OK.* But as I lay there, Stella's eyes looked like those of my Grandma Patricia, my own personal patron saint of unconditional love. She loved animals. She loved me. She loved virtually everybody, the proverbial peacekeeper. Always looking for the best in people.

I know, strange. All I know is that I soon drifted off to one of the best nights of sleep I'd had in a long time. When I woke up, Stella hadn't moved. She'd stayed by my side all night long, the first time she'd done that. I hadn't been used to such loyalty—and that night, it may have saved my life.

THE UNIVERSITY OF Oregon soon hired me back as its associate director of development. They knew what happened in Fresno. They'd read the stories. They'd talked to people. And they hired me anyway. The university offered me counseling for my PTSD. Individuals called me, brought me food, asked what they could do to help. One of the most common text messages I got was: "Call me if you need help in any way." It all made me feel like you do when taking a hot shower after being out in the cold.

Life, I was reminded, is about relationships—and I was honored to be welcomed home by people whose links to me were so strong that they did so with open arms, despite my baggage. I found a new counselor in Eugene—a wonderful counselor—and started pulling all the tools out of the toolbox to deal with my PTSD: from yoga to meditation, diet to exercise, healthy eating to—I love this one—returning to my happy place.

I started returning to Convict Lake on a regular basis, at least in my mind; it not only provided a distraction but offered possibilities—the hopes of "real live" Convict Lake moments in the future. And I began thinking about not only speaking to groups around the country about childhood sex abuse but telling my own story as well. The result, of course, is this book.

In some ways, my life had come full circle, back to the place I got my start nearly twenty-five years before. Then, suddenly, that life was in danger. In 2018, at age fifty-three, my weight plummeted from 165 to 125. While in Berkeley for an Oregon-California football game, my kidneys and liver began showing signs of shutting down. Phil and Penny arranged for me to be admitted to the Stanford University Medical Center.

Before I knew it, doctors were talking about liver and kidney transplants. Basically, they told me that my body had "shut down" as the result of a number of factors: the culmination of trauma, stress, poor diet, lack of exercise, and a family history of kidney and liver problems.

My mother was at my bedside. A priest was praying with me, which, for obvious reasons, I found as unsettling as comforting. This was a far more serious manifestation of the stress-induced afflictions I'd suffered nearly twenty years before, first experienced on a trip back from a football game in Hawaii. Fortunately, with antibiotics and fluids, I improved markedly in the next few days. I was transferred to OHSU in Portland

and continued to get better. But when released I was basically told I needed to slow down, eat better, and exercise more. Otherwise, a third storm of such symptoms could prove fatal.

It felt good to finally be back home in Eugene. In the previous few years, I had learned a lot about people, much of it coming not in the spotlight of news conferences but in the nooks and crannies of Sierra Tucson and of Passages, where I met so many people with the courage to look in the mirror with an eye toward self-knowledge instead of shame, get real with themselves, and become better versions of who they'd been.

I had learned what it's like, for once, to not be the guy trying to save everybody else, but to be the guy who needed saving. In that respect, to read the letters that poured in when I went public with my abuse, to exchange encouragement with the guys from the Warrior Lodge, to sit across from a good friend who accepts me for who I am, despite my struggles—such things reminded me of my worth despite people who've tried to convince me otherwise.

I had learned how powerful it can be when one person looks at another not as an employee or a spouse or a pawn or homeless or liberal or conservative or any other label we might want to slap on them, but just as a fellow human being, sharing the same planet. And how powerful it can be when we react with compassion. Once, back in Eugene, a friend called me and said, "How you doing, Jimmy?" We talked for a few minutes. I started wondering why he'd called, what he needed from me. But then I realized: He just wanted to know how I was doing, just wanted to make sure I was OK. *Blew me away.*

Finally, I had learned that some people in positions of power will go to great lengths to control others. It happened in the rectory in Pinole. It happened at Fresno State. But in the aftermath of the Fresno State debacle, I decided I, for one, refuse to be defined by Stephen Kiesle or anyone else who considers only their own best interests and not the interests of others.

As Elton John sings in his song *I'm Still Standing: Don't you know I'm still standing better than I ever did/Looking like a true survivor, feeling like a little kid.*

That's me. I'm still standing.

I'm not one of those people who believes that, given a second chance, they'd "choose to live their life just as they did." I've wished a million times that I'd never met Kiesle and that I'd never been through the hell he put me and all the other children through. But I can't change that. As the Serenity Prayer says: "God, grant me the serenity to accept the things I cannot change, Courage to change the things I can, And wisdom to know the difference." What I can change is how I live my life going forward. Unless we're perpetrators such as Kiesle, we are all victims, survivors, or beneficiaries of our circumstances. I choose *survivor*.

I believe in grace, in forgiveness, in letting the past go. I also believe in justice, which is why I filed a claim against Fresno State that was settled out of court. But I remain honored to have served the university. I will forever be grateful for President Castro for giving me the opportunity I had at the university and will forever be proud of what I was able to accomplish, particularly in regard to the turnaround in the all-important football program. Though we didn't see eye-to-eye regarding the job I was doing, I respect President Castro's commitment to education, I respect his family, and I wish him well.

Looking back, perhaps my situation was so unlike anything the university had ever dealt with that they simply had no idea how to react. How to help. What I needed. I get it: when you work for someone, it's a two-way street. Your employer rightfully expects something from you and you rightfully expect something from them. But have we become so cold as society that human compassion has no place in the equation?

I don't regret for a moment going public with my abuse. I was saddened that we'd once had the synchronization but lost it. I regret that the Fresno State job didn't work out. That it ended so badly. That I didn't get the chance to stay and help make a great university even greater. But any bitterness I'd had about that situation is now gone—and I remain a die-hard Bulldog fan, thankful for the chance to put a piece in the university's rebuilding project.

But on the Catholic Church front, there's a difference between forgiving someone and forgetting. That I'm still a practicing Catholic confirms my willingness to forgive the Church. I don't believe the unconscionable actions of a few should negate the honorable lives of millions. My children have spent their entire lives being educated in Catholic schools and I believe it's taught them leadership, responsibility, and serving others. Though I am not a regular in the pews, I still find sustenance in the Catholic faith.

That said, the Church has protected its own for far too long—at the expense of innocent victims and their families. People who have been forgiven must nevertheless be held accountable for their actions.

After I went public, among the few e-mails I got from detractors, interestingly, was one from a Catholic priest. My paraphrase: "Jim, what you need to show to the Catholic Church is not your anger, but your compassion."

How *dare* he. I'm abused by a Catholic priest for three years at the most vulnerable, formative time of my life—a betrayal that smudges every day of my life with a blotch of darkness—and the responsibility is *mine* to make everything right? The message was as clear as the message that had haunted me nearly every night: *It's your fault!*

I was incredulous at his insensitivity. Unfortunately, that's the pattern that abuse victims often face; it's the basketball equivalent of a defender standing his or her ground, being knocked hard to the floor by an out-of-control offensive player driving to the basket, then being whistled for a foul. Like it's *our* fault that grown men repeatedly raped us, then lied and said they didn't. And the church covered for them.

Where has the Catholic Church been in *my* healing process? Nowhere. Yes, I need to focus on compassion but starting—as therapy has taught me—with self-confession, which helps ground me in compassion for others. But in the three years since I went public with the abuse, not one church official—despite my getting national attention—has personally reached out to me and offered even a smidgen of empathy. Catholic teachers, friends, colleagues? Yes. But leaders? No. Not a peep.

It is time the Catholic Church stopped hiding behind its cloak of pompous traditions and showed the integrity, honor, and compassion of the Jesus they profess to follow. Time to see sexual abuse through the eyes of individual victims, not the church's public relations firm. Time to do the right damn thing. *Now.*

Meanwhile, I'm doing my part to seek justice not only for me, but for all who've been sexually abused: In March 2020, under a new California law that widens the time window for those claiming to have been sexually abused to seek compensation for damages, I filed a lawsuit against the Archdiocese of Oakland, California.

Lawsuits aren't the perfect mechanism for justice, but for victims they're the only tangible symbol of justice available. What we need isn't million-dollar payments for past sins, but people in power positions to do what I've spent a lifetime doing: facing themselves in the mirror. It's priests with the integrity to walk the "consider-others-more-important-than-yourself" talk; a Vatican that defends the "least of these" instead of continually covering the sins of its leaders; and people in positions of power to not defend sexual abusers by reassigning them but reporting them to law-enforcement officials so justice may be served.

Meanwhile, victims need to muster the courage to step forward and report when they think someone has touched them inappropriately in any way. I kept silent far too long—and I regret that. How many children suffered what I did because I didn't dare speak up?

As for perpetrators, the best we can hope for is enough ethical insight to expect from themselves the same thing they expect from others. To stay away from whatever doesn't belong to them. And to understand that what might be a trivial pursuit to themselves can ruin the lives—even *end* the lives, given the suicides we see—of their victims.

As for Kiesle, I'd like him to read a book. It's called *Boy in the Mirror*. It's about a little boy who was taken prisoner, in a sense, by a priest. But, in the end, the little boy grows up, breaks free, and finds the same courage that the female victim had found back in the early 2000s—the courage to tell her story, which led to the priest going to prison for six years. It took a while for the kid to muster that courage—more than four decades—and it cost him plenty. A wife. A relationship with his daughter, who's struggled to process, at a tender age, what this all means. A job as an athletic director of a major university, the pinnacle of my long, dedicated career in the world of sports. A reputation. And a helluva lot of sleep.

But in the end the priest loses. Though freed from prison in 2010, he winds up in chains of his own making, shackled to a truth that abides even if he can't see it: he spent most of his life—and perhaps still spends it—exploiting the weak. It is a sad legacy. In the lexicon of sports, it is the legacy of a loser. In the rectory back in the mid-'70s, he would warn Robbie and I that if we told, the monster would be unleashed—on the little boy and his friend. But, in the end, we learned that the monster wasn't outside. He was right there, in the room with us. And, in the end, the monster dies. Devours himself with his own greed, having spent his entire life feeding his selfishness and misses the wonder of giving to something beyond himself. What a pity. As author Richelle E. Goodrich says, "A monster's worst fear is of being found."

AND THE LITTLE boy? He wins. He tells his story and, in so doing, is reminded that it was never his fault to begin with. He refuses to take responsibility for the priest's cruelty. And realizes that all the pain, turmoil, and betrayal he's experienced has helped him see a deeper side to life. Deeper than wins and losses. Soul stuff.

He learns to value life differently. Embraces friends and family more deeply—*relationships*. Sees differently. He still loves sports, but at a night football game at Autzen Stadium he looks beyond the action on the field and the scoreboard to the beauty of a half-moon hanging high above the field in a splendor that can't be matched below. And thinks of the 17th-century Japanese poet and samurai, Mizuta Masahide, who said, "My barn having burned down, I can now see the moon."

His perspective on life has changed. At age fifty-four, in June 2019, he flies to the Bay Area, meets a friend, rents a car, drives to Pinole, and looks at the rectory where it happened. He walks into the church next door. He runs his hand along the wall in the St. Joseph School gym where Father Steve threw basketballs at him to punish him for committing turnovers. Finally, he drives to the gated community where his abuser lives and tries his best to talk the guard into letting him pass; he wants to knock at the man's door and see if the former priest still remembers him. Say hello. And ask one question: why?

In other words, instead of running away from the abuse—and its ghost—like he'd felt necessary his whole life, he faces it. He drives to his old house on Diablo Court in Pinole, the place where he would take his baseball bat out into the side yard and let his imagination transport him to Dodger Stadium, a place where he could be anything he wanted to be. The house is empty; nobody's living there now. He walks around the north side, where the baseball games took place.

For a moment, on this June afternoon, he sees where the boyhood games were once played and smiles, taking it all in like a flower-lover might breathe in the fragrance of a fresh-cut bouquet. Like a man recharging from a time before the innocence was shattered. Like a man embracing an optimism for the future that's as wide as his imagination can dream.

May 1975. It's the bottom of the ninth inning and Los Angeles is down 4-3 to the Cubs at Dodger Stadium. The Dodgers need a run to tie and two to win. But there's hope in the air because Los Angeles bats last.

Just like the little boy.

Epilogue

In February 2013, Pope Benedict XVI resigned as head of the Catholic Church, citing a "lack of strength of mind and body" due to advancing age. He was eighty-five.

In May 2019, A.J. graduated from Loyola-Marymount and, having served as an intern at Price-Waterhouse, was offered a full-time job at the major accounting and finance firm. Danielle, a high school junior in Fresno, has played on her high school's varsity tennis team since she was a freshman and done well in the classroom. Now seventeen, she is no longer the little girl I remembered but has blossomed into a beautiful and bright young woman who makes her father proud.

On October 13, 2019, California Governor Gavin Newsom signed into law a bill that increases the statute of limitations on filing legal actions for childhood sexual assault by fourteen years—from the time an alleged victim is twenty-six years old to age forty—and extends the period for delayed reasonable discovery claims from three to five years. It also allows a window of three years for the revival of past claims that might have expired due to the statute of limitations. The bill passed the California State Assembly 69-0 and the Senate 33-0.

In December 2019, the divorce between Eileen and me was finalized. Agreeing on a settlement was bitter, this having dragged on for more than two years. I felt relief, sadness, anger, regret, disappointment—nearly every emotion possible. But I was thankful knowing I could at least now move forward without this weight on me. I was not thankful for the way the settlement landed. "Thanks," Eileen's attorney said to me when the hearing was over, "it was great doing business with you." I hadn't considered it business. I'd considered it my life, Eileen's life, our children's lives. But it's time to move forward.

In early 2020 I was privileged to be welcomed into a partnership with the University of Oregon's Center for the Prevention of Abuse and Neglect—part of UO's College of Education— and its "90by30" initiative. In addition, through the UO, I've established the Jimmy Bartko Scholarship fund, donations to which will go to helping prevent child sexual abuse and to help students who've been abused attend the University of Oregon.

Meanwhile, I'd been in therapy for more than three years to understand ways to cope with my sexual abuse. Working with therapists in Malibu, California, and Eugene, I've come to understand myself better than ever before. Am I "healed?" No. I don't ever expect to completely get over the trauma I've faced. But, meanwhile, I'm still standing.

Afterword

To Readers in General

I'm often asked if I'd do it again—go public with my abuse. Yes. Without question. Not that it's been easy; in some ways, it was a catalyst for making my life hell. It led to my divorce and to being forced to resign from Fresno State. But I've begun to trust my instincts and to realize that when I see a red flag in how someone labels or caricatures me, it says more about them than it does about me. And here's what overrides all the pain I've been through: in the mirror each night, I can look myself in the eye. I can live each day knowing that I've taken a stand against a wrong that our society has ignored for far too long. And I can know that, if even in a small way, I've helped others get beyond their own abuse.

Before I left the facility in Arizona where I first shared about my past, my therapist, Mary, suggested I do four things:

- **First, send a letter to yourself as a child.** *Check.* Until going through therapy, I never understood that the pit in my stomach I so often felt was a little boy desperately trying to be heard. I wish I hadn't waited so long to listen to him. It was a hard letter to write but wonderfully rewarding. Together, the two of us finally found our happy place.

- **Second, reconnect with your best childhood friend, Robbie.** *Check.* He was almost always abused in the same incidents I was. When I moved from Pinole, however, I didn't see him again for more than forty years. When we reunited, I didn't know where to start. But I was pleasantly surprised to find our relationship hardly skipped a beat. It's rewarding to have him, his sister Teri and brother Tommy back in my life. We share so many painful memories. And, like me, he has battled the effects every day. But he's winning that battle now and I'm blessed to be able to lean on his strength in my tough times. As noted in the book, we disagree on only one thing—"survivor" terminology. I call the two of us "survivors." He simply says, "we survived." We both have friends and family to cherish, and both plan to do what we can do to help others lost in the rubble of abuse. Thank you, Robbie and Teri, for being there for me; please know that I will always be there for you.

- **Third, decide for myself how, or if, I want to disclose my abuse to others.** *Check.* My choice was to be bold and go public with it. I lived a lie most of my life; now I feel honored to help others who've been through what I've been through, and to perhaps help some children avoid what I've been through. Whether it's one person or one thousand, I want to make a difference. To that end, I plan to speak regularly on the issue. I've already accepted an offer from the University of Oregon's Center for the Prevention of Abuse and Neglect to partner with them on helping stop child abuse through its "90by30" initiative. And I've started the Jimmy Bartko Scholarship Fund to help support such an effort.

- **Fourth, tell your story.** *Check.* If you've gotten this far, you probably just read my story. It's amazing what you learn about yourself when you dare examine yourself up close. This process has given me clarity, addressed the guilt and shame I felt, and changed my perspective on how I live. Writing this book has been like an eighteen-month "teachable moment," among the lessons that words are powerful. The headlines in the *Fresno Bee*. The comments students have made to my daughter. The things people whisper behind your back. Words hurt.

I now wake up each day with hope and a smile. Perhaps even more crucially, I'm sleeping better than I have since I was six. "Night" and "anxiety" are no longer synonymous.

Do I still have tough moments? Absolutely, but I also have family and friends who have showed me the care and understanding we all need. I'm excited for my next life chapter, even if I'm unsure just where it will take me.

Meanwhile, I have only two regrets:

First, that I didn't tell about what Steve Kiesle did to me immediately after the first incident; I still wonder how many children would have avoided such trauma had I told my parents about the abuse and they would have reported it to the police.

And, second, that my children, A.J. and Danielle, have had to go through their own emotional trauma because of my going public with the abuse: the breakup of their parents' marriage, the questions they've had to endure from others, the embarrassment I know they've felt.

I'm sorry.

Had I stayed silent you probably wouldn't have had to go through what you have. But that's a bell I can't un-ring. I hope that this book will help you better understand the "why" behind that decision and I hope that you will never forget this: I love you both unconditionally and will always be there for you.

To Fellow Survivors of
Childhood Sexual Abuse in Particular

In 2018, the National Police Agency recorded 80,000-plus reports of child abuse. There are now nearly one million Registered Sex Offenders in the United States. Here in my home state of Oregon, of 25,000 people who participated in a Stewards of Children/Protect Our Children program, thirty-two percent indicated they had been sexually abused in childhood.

Given such gut-churning statistics, I'd be remiss if I didn't look in the eye of every survivor of childhood sexual abuse and tell you what I've learned and say: I'm sorry for what you've gone through and what you must live with. Some of you offer heartwarming stories of success, others can't seem to outrun the past. We all come from different backgrounds and different stories, but we are bonded by our common struggle. May you bury the monster and find the happiness that's long overdue you.

Always remember this:

- **First, it's not your fault.** Others might give you that impression. Some may have told you outright you're to blame. And maybe you've told yourself that. But nobody has the right to touch your body without your permission and "informed consent," something no child is old enough to give. I'd say "forgive yourself" but that suggests you did something wrong. You didn't. You're not the bad guy here. Your abuser is. Cast off any guilt or shame you might be feeling.

- **Second, talk to people who can help.** Like me, you might think carrying the secret is the right way to go—or your cross to bear—but you're carrying a burden that isn't yours to carry. If you can afford it, get professional counseling. If you can't, explore options for therapy from nonprofits and other more affordable options.

- **Third, consider joining a group therapy program that deals specifically with victims of childhood sexual abuse.**

- **Fourth, realize you don't have to be chained to the past.** In short, your history is not your destiny. My therapist in Eugene has these words from Carl Jung on her business card: "I am not what happened to me. I am what I choose to become."

- **Fifth, involve yourself with other people.** Just because one person hurt you doesn't mean all people are bad. Relationships can be a tremendous comfort. Have the courage to risk fostering good relationships with the kind of people who aren't going to think less of you because of what happened to you in the past. Be wary of those who do.

- **Sixth, stay positive, stay healthy, and don't let the monster devour you.**

- **And, finally, don't be afraid to start over.** It's scary. It's unknown. But as mythology guru Joseph Campbell says: "We must be willing to get rid of the life we've planned, so as to have the life that is waiting for us."

Fighting Childhood Sexual Abuse

Because I feel so strongly about this issue, I've asked the co-founders of the University of Oregon's Center for the Prevention of Abuse and Neglect to offer readers some perspective on the subject. The center's largest project, the "90by30" initiative, seeks to reduce child abuse in the county where UO is located—Lane County—by 90% by 2030. Here are their thoughts:

It is an important moment when survivors break their silence to talk about their experiences, especially when it is done, as it is here, in part to support other survivors who may or may not have ever talked about what happened to them. This book gives each of us an opportunity to pause—take a minute to really think about this issue, informed by what we know and by what we learned from Jim' story.

What we know is that there are millions of survivors of child sexual abuse in our country who go forward each day in their own ways of coping with past trauma. Some may self-medicate, while others may suffer from depression or anxiety or even PTSD.

What we also know is that each and every time a survivor "discloses," it is an opportunity to acknowledge them and what they went through, an opportunity to be a part of breaking the silence.

What we also know is that it is imperative to be good listeners when a survivor tells us about his or her experience. No matter how close or far from the experience the listener is, every disclosure is an opportunity for us to be a part of the healing—in how we respond, how we acknowledge, and how we thank them for sharing and breaking that silence. It is also an opportunity to refrain from common—and harmful—responses, such as asking questions that could imply blame, such as "Why did you go to his house?"

In addition to the key role we play as support to survivors in our midst, we can also play a key role in the prevention of child abuse and neglect. Central to this role is working together to change the factors, in particular the culture of silence that allows child abuse to persist. In Lane County, Oregon, among high school junior and senior survivors of child abuse and neglect, 47% reported they have never shared their trauma with anyone (Todahl, Barkhurst, & Schnabler, 2019). This is no accident. The social norms that trap survivors in silence fuel the persistence of child abuse in our communities.

The prevention of child abuse, certainly, demands intentional and community-wide action. Jim's story is a call to action.

There is reason for optimism. Some of us have power over policies and can ensure, for example, that in youth-serving organizations, churches and schools, that no child is left alone with an adult unless they are in a visible and public setting. Moreover, educating children, youth and adults about safe touch, consent, and healthy relationships counters silence and promotes safety and connection. Shared efforts to raise awareness, change social norms, and identify specific action plans are making a difference. By some reports, rates of intimate partner violence (domestic violence) in the United States have declined steadily over the past forty years (Fox & Fridel, 2017).

Community-based and primary prevention efforts are highly promising. For example, in Lane County, Oregon, the University of Oregon is partnering with residents in a community-led effort to reduce child abuse by 90%. Child abuse is preventable; we can move from it being close to the rule, to being the exception. Our community-campus partnership, known as the 90by30 Initiative, works to change the culture of silence by putting the work of child abuse prevention in the hands of all community members. It is a holistic, locally made plan with a central message: The protection of children is a shared core adult responsibility; we all have a role. Our work is pointing to practical actions each of us can take (e.g., http://knowmorelanecounty.org). We encourage you to review our effort. It is making a difference in our community.

On behalf of Jim and all survivors, we hope it will be useful in yours.

Phyllis D. Barkhurst
Jeff Todahl
Co-Directors, Center for the Prevention of Abuse and Neglect
College of Education, University of Oregon

Acknowledgments

The one constant in my story has been the family and friends who've stood by me. It's a sad truth that you learn who your true friends are in times of struggle. I can never repay all of you for what you've done for me in this, the most difficult time of my life. You've stuck with me, listened to me, shown compassion to me. You've never doubted me. In short, you've helped save my life. I thank you from the deepest places of my heart. And I vow I will pay your respect to me forward as I invest in the lives of others.

Thank you to the people who've been there with me, like no others, through thick and thin: Mom and Dad; my sister, Kim Abel; Phil and Penny Knight; and Robbie.

To my two children, A.J., and Danielle. I'm sorry that as "innocent angels," you got pulled into this mess. I'm sorry for the pain you've had to go through. I hope as you grow up, you'll have a better understanding of what all this means. Meanwhile, I love you both from the bottom of my heart and I will be there for you forever.

Thanks to so many others:

To those who helped me write this book: Bob Welch, my co-writer who helped bring the story to life; Ron Bellamy, who believed in my idea, encouraged me to write the book, and gave our rough drafts a couple of reads; Tinker Hatfield, who threw his heart and soul into the cover drawing; Ann Petersen, who edited our original version; Jeff Wright and Mark Johnson, who copyedited semifinal and final versions of the manuscript, respectively; and to the following people who read the manuscript and offered suggestions: Ken Woody, Rick Simons, Robbie, Stu McDowell, Pat Kilkenny, Renee Baumgartner, Tim Younger, and Carolyn Taylor.

To Uncle Dan Johnson and Aunt Ruby. And to the rest of my sister Kim's family: Keith, Melissa, Michaela, Ellie, and Marcus.

To those friends who've especially been with me since I "crossed the chalked line": Brad Bills, Jeff Todahl, Kristi Morris Schneider, Judge Mike Hogan, Rick Harder, Heidi Pollock, Joe and Janine Gonyea, Steve and Sally Lee, Neil and Stephanie Everett, Peter Jacobsen, J Torchio, Joey Harrington, Carolyn Taylor, Dave and Lynn Frohnmayer, Mike and Sheila Schwartz, Allan Price, Julia Grace Visanopky, Passages of Malibu, Sierra Tucson, Rick Simons, Robbie Rosson, Teri Rosson, Kelly Stonebreaker, Lisa McKillips, Tim Younger, Kit Morris, Rob Mullens, Mike Andreason, Tom Wuest, Roger Orth, Marvin Adams, Roger George, Gary Janzen, Beth Dunn, Jill Kirby, Harold Reynolds, Jeff Hawkins, Vin Lananna, the Wildish Family, the Papé Family, John and Linda Harrison, Dan Guistina, Ed and Cyndy Maletis, John Canzano, Alberto Salazar, Galen Rupp, Geoff Walker, Jim and Tracy Morse, Mike and Colleen Bellotti, Roxy Bernstein, Stanford University Medical Center, Oregon Health & Sciences University, Oak Street Medical: Allergy and Asthma, Glenn Keiper, Denny and Carey McNally, Pat and Stephanie Kilkenny, Kit Morris, Leslie Fisher, Franklin and Brittany Alegria, Jim and Mary Jaqua, Davey Walton, and Downstream. (And to the few who I will have somehow overlooked in my rush to make a book deadline after eighteen months of work. You know who you are. Please know I appreciate you.)

To those who are partnering with me to help stop child abuse and to help young people who've been abused attend the University of Oregon: Phyllis D. Barkhurst and Jeff Todahl, founders and directors of the Center for the Prevention of Abuse and Neglect, and President Michael Schill.

To those who defend children, particularly Maurine Behrend, the Diocese of Oakland youth leader who dared to ask why Kiesle was still involved with children after he'd already been convicted of child molestation: thank you for having the courage to call out those who need calling out.

To Stella, my beloved dog: Girl, you are what loyalty is all about.

Finally, to the boy in the mirror: Thank you for having the courage to cross that *Field of Dreams* line. Even though you can never go back to who you were, may you find comfort in knowing that, even if later than you'd wished, your stepping forward might save even one child from the trauma you endured. If so, this book will have been worth it.

Contact information

To contact me, particularly about speaking to your organization, school or business: boyinthemirror@gmail.com

To get more information about the 90by30 initiative go to: knowmorelanecounty.org

To contribute to the Jimmy Bartko Scholarship Fund, or the Prevention of Abuse and Neglect fund, contact Kristi Schneider at the UO's College of Education at kristim@uoregon.edu

Other organizations I recommend to help children include:

- The Bald Faced Truth Foundation provides opportunities for children in art, music, education, and athletics. It was founded by John Canzano, *Oregonian* columnist and 740 AM "The Game" radio talk-show host. Info: baldfacedtruth. org

- Hosea Youth Services. A Eugene, Oregon, organization that

helps high-risk and homeless young people build healthy lives away from the streets. Info: www.hoseayouth.org

- KidSports, a Eugene, Oregon, youth sports organization that provides "positive youth team sports experiences through family and community involvement." Info: kidsports.org

- Food Security Project at Fresno State University. Supports students who may be "experiencing food insecurity and other challenges" with resources to help meet their needs. Info: www.fresnostate.edu/studentaffairs/foodsecurity

Appendix

Cardinal Ratzinger's letter to Diocese of Oakland Bishop John S. Cummings

Following is the text of a November 1985 letter, signed by then-Cardinal —and future Pope—Joseph Ratzinger, to Oakland Bishop John S. Cummins. The subject is Father Steve Kiesle's wish to be defrocked—three years after being found guilty of child molestation in connection with two boys being tied up and sexually assaulted. Cummins supported the idea.

The letter, originally written in Latin, was translated for The Associated Press by Thomas Habinek, chairman of the University of Southern California Classics Department.

Most Excellent Bishop

Having received your letter of September 13 of this year, regarding the matter of the removal from all priestly burdens pertaining to Rev. Stephen Miller Kiesle in your diocese, it is my duty to share with you the following:

This court, although it regards the arguments presented in favor of removal in this case to be of grave significance, nevertheless deems it necessary to consider the good of the Universal Church together with that of the petitioner, and it is also unable to make light of the detriment that granting the dispensation can provoke with the community of Christ's faithful, particularly regarding the young age of the petitioner.

It is necessary for this Congregation to submit incidents of this sort to very careful consideration, which necessitates a longer period of time.

In the meantime your Excellency must not fail to provide the petitioner with as much paternal care as possible and in addition to explain to same the rationale of this court, which is accustomed to proceed keeping the common good especially before its eyes.

Let me take this occasion to convey sentiments of the highest regard always to you.

Your most Reverend Excellency

    Joseph Cardinal Ratzinger

Steve Kiesle Timeline

A timeline of defrocked priest Stephen Kiesle, the man who sexually abused Jim Bartko and, says attorney Rick Simons, more than 200 other children:

- **1972:** Ordained at St. Francis De Sales, Oakland.
- **1972-1975:** Associate pastor at St. Joseph's Church in Pinole.

- **1975-1978**: Assigned to Our Lady of the Rosary in Union City.

- **August 1978:** Kiesle is arrested and pleads no contest to lewd conduct, a misdemeanor, for tying up and molesting two boys. Sentenced to three years probation, record is later expunged.

- **1978-1981:** Takes extended leave of absence, attends counseling and reports regularly to probation officer.

- **July 1981**: Oakland Bishop John Cummins sends Kiesle's file to the Vatican in support of Kiesle's petition for laicization, or being removed as a priest.

- **November 1981:** Vatican asks for more information.

- **1982:** Kiesle moves to Pinole.

- **February 1982:** Cummins writes to Ratzinger providing additional information and warning of possible scandal if Kiesle is not defrocked.

- **September 1982:** Oakland diocese official writes Ratzinger asking for update.

- **September 1983:** Cummins visits Rome, discusses Kiesle case with Vatican officials.

- **December 1983:** Vatican official writes Oakland to say Kiesle's file can't be found and they should resubmit materials.

- **January 1984:** Cummins writes a Vatican official to inquire about status of Kiesle file.

- **1985:** Kiesle volunteers as a youth minister at St. Joseph's Church in Pinole.

- **September 1985:** Cummins writes Ratzinger asking about status of Kiesle case.

- **November 1985:** Ratzinger writes to Cummins about Kiesle case.

- **December 1985:** A memo from diocese officials discusses writing to Ratzinger again to stress the risk of scandal if Kiesle's case is delayed.

- **1987:** Kiesle is defrocked.

- **2002:** Kiesle is arrested and charged with 13 counts of child molestation; all but two are thrown out after U.S. Supreme Court ruling invalidates a California law extending statute of limitations.

- **2004:** Kiesle pleads no contest to felony charge of molesting a young girl in 1995 at his Truckee vacation home.

- **2004:** He is sentenced to six years in prison for the 1995 molestation.

- **2010:** Registered as a sex offender living in a gated retirement community in Walnut Creek, California.

Resources
Books

Bass, E., & Davis, L. (1988). *The Courage to Heal: A Guide for Women Survivors of Child Sexual Abuse.* Perennial Library/Harper & Row Publishers.

Berry, Jason. *Leads Us Not into Temptation: Catholic Priests and the Sexual Abuse of Children.*

Bradshaw, John. (1988.) *Bradshaw on: Healing the Shame that Binds you.* Deerfield, FL: Health Communications. First LevelFiveMedia.

Brown, Brené. (2010.) *The Gifts of Imperfection: Let Go of Who You Think You're Supposed to Be and Embrace Who You Are.* Center City, MN: Hazeldon.

Burke-Harris, N. (2018). *The Deepest Well: Healing the Long-Term Effects of Childhood Adversity.* London: Bluebird.

Emerson, D., & Hopper, E. (2011). *Overcoming Trauma Through Yoga: Reclaiming Your Body.* Berkeley: North Atlantic Books.

Freyd, J. (1996). *Betrayal Trauma: The Logic of Forgetting Childhood Abuse.* Harvard University Press.

Groves, B. (2002). *Children Who See Too Much.* Boston: Beacon Press.

Herman, J. (2015). *Trauma and Recovery: The Aftermath of*

Violence—from Domestic Abuse to Political Terror. New York: Basic Books.

Hindman, J. (1989). *Just before dawn: From the shadows of tradition to new reflections in trauma assessment and treatment of sexual victims.* Alexandria Associates.

Hindman, J. (1991). *101 "Proactive" Treatment strategies breaking the bonds of trauma for victims of sexual abuse.* Alexandria Associates.

Hindman, J. (1983). *A very touching book: For little people and for big people.* Alexandria Associates.

Lamott, Anne. (1994.) Bird by Bird: Some Instructions on Writing and Life. New York: Anchor.

Levine, P., & Phillips, M. (2012). *Freedom from Pain: Discover Your Body's Power to Overcome Physical Pain.* Boulder, CO: Sounds True.

Maltz, W. (2012). *The Sexual Healing Journey: A Guide for Survivors of Sexual Abuse* (3rd ed). New York: Harper Collins.

Neff, Kristin. (2015.) *Self-Compassion: The Proven Power of Being Kind to Yourself.* New York: William Morrow.

Van der Kolk, B. (2014). *The Body Keeps the Score: Brain, Mind, and Body in the Healing of Trauma.* New York: Penguin Books.

Sege, R., Bethell, C., Linkenbach, J., Jones, J., Klika, B., & Pecora, P. (2017). *Balancing Adverse Childhood Experiences (ACEs) With HOPE: New Insights into the Role of Positive Experience on Child and Family Development.* Casey Family Programs

Websites

Faith Communities

United States Conference of Catholic Bishops – Catholic Church Action on Child Sexual Abuse Prevention:

http://www.usccb.org/about/child-and-youth-protection/index.cfm

Faith Trust Institute:

http://www.faithtrustinstitute.org/

The Faith Trust Institute is a national, multifaith, multicultural training and education organization working to end sexual and domestic violence.

General

Male Survivor.
https://malesurvivor.org

Institute on Violence, Abuse and Trauma (IVAT):
https://www.ivatcenters.org

Our Whole Lives: A healthy sexuality curriculum:
https://www.ucc.org/justice_sexuality-education_our-whole-lives

Prevention, Support and Information
for Survivors and Friends

National Sexual Assault Hotline. Free. Confidential. 24/7:
1-800-656-HOPE

National Sexual Violence Resource Center:
https://www.nsvrc.org

Rape, Abuse and Incest National Network – RAINN:
https://www.rainn.org

Futures Without Violence:
https://www.futureswithoutviolence.org

National Domestic Violence Hotline:
https://www.thehotline.org; 1–800–799–7233

For Youth: Is my relationship safe and healthy?
https://www.loveisrespect.org

I am concerned about a friend or family member:
https://www.thehotline.org/help/help-for-friends-and-family/

Support for Survivors of Sexual Abuse :
sass-lane.org

Darkness to Light:
https://www.d2l.org

Adverse Childhood Experiences: Hope and Resilience:

https://cssp.org/resource/balancing-aces-with-hope-final/

National Suicide Prevention Lifeline:
1-800-273-8255